ANNIE FALK DAVIS

D1827432

SUICIDE AWARENESS

A MOTHER'S WARNING

outskirts
press

ACKNOWLEDGMENT

THANK YOU

To God, in whom I have never lost faith.

To my husband, Rod, for his quiet strength, his patience, his protective arms always ready to hold me and his hand to squeeze when the horrifying flashbacks of finding my son dead in our bathtub suddenly played before my eyes.

To my daughters, Sue and Sandy, for whom I kept my will to live, regardless of the shock that my life would never be the same.

To my grandchildren, who brought the gentle baby love back into my life.

To our son, Michael, for giving us twenty-one special and fulfilling years of pride and the unique depth of the love between a mother and her son.

TABLE OF CONTENTS

PREFACE

This book is dedicated to the son we lost at age 21 to a terminal illness called "Undetected Depression and Anxiety." Someone we called "Worrywart," Michael was not living a thousand miles away; he was not silent; he was not losing weight; he never cried; he was not irritable. He was sleeping in his bedroom next to ours; going to school (or so we thought). He was expressing his anguish over recent complications in his transfer from Alabama to Texas. And we were listening. We were encouraging. We were giving love and attention, strokes, thoughts, opinions, suggestions and advice. Not just occasionally, but daily-several times a day. Where did we go wrong? Timing. We knew nothing about depression or anxiety. It wasn't publicly discussed. It wasn't privately discussed.

Can you even imagine what it is like to wake up one day and know you will never see your wonderful son or daughter again as long as you live? Could you handle being reminded of your loss every time a memory slams into your fragile existence? Can you feel the devastation of going to events where your child or young adult should have been in school, sports, church, graduation, family gatherings, wedding, or other people's funerals? Not just at the time of your youth's death, but for the rest of your living days?

Depression and anxiety creep in unknown, unseen and like an

addiction or disease, seems to take ahold of a part of the brain, choking off past reasoning abilities, rational future plans and the contentment of the present.

Why else would a healthy, loving, caring, gentle, intelligent, talented, wonderful boy/man turn around and leave his mom, who was his best friend growing up; his dad who was his athletic buddy; his sisters with whom he shared great times, his grandma, who was his "Woobi," his girlfriend, whom he thought he would someday marry, and all of his friends he schooled with, rough housed with, fielded with and laughed with—KILL HIMSELF?

I am writing this book with the hope that after all that I have read, written about and reflected on for more than 20 years I can stop a young person before suicide becomes the choice of a very preventable disease. After writing in my journal for six years, I couldn't just put it in a drawer without trying to warn a mom about all the obvious signs of mental distress and seeking professional help immediately. And sadly, if her child has already completed suicide, how to survive the catastrophe.

Most importantly, for those left behind, how to find direction and purpose—that which my son gradually lost in four months before my very unseeing eyes.

The Lord is close to the brokenhearted and saves those who are crushed in spirit. Psalm 34;18

CHAPTER ONE

FIRST DAY OF THE REST OF MY LIFE

IT WASN'T THE start of a typical day. My husband, Rod, nudged me at 5 a.m. and whispered, "Are you asleep?" "No, why?" I whispered back. "You want to go fishing?" "God, yes!" And there in the midst of darkness, on a mild, mid-September Saturday in 1994, my decision terminally ended 54 years of my blessed and happy life.

The day before, Rod and I were on our office home phones, negotiating and processing eleven sales of properties in rapidly growing Plano, Texas. We needed a break from the stress of working eighty-hour work weeks, so the idea of fishing peacefully an hour away at Lake Texoma seemed heavenly.

I tiptoed into my 21-year-old son's room. The light from the hall fell on his long, slender, athletic body, clad only in his soft and faded green, plaid boxer shorts. I whispered, "Honey, do you want to go to Texoma and fish with us?" I caught a glimpse of his dimples that I so loved, as he rolled over with a sleepy grin.

"Can't Mom, Bill and I are watching the football game this afternoon."

"Ok," I said. "We'll be back around five." As I kissed his cheek, he murmured, "Love ya, Mom."

"Love you, Mike." He turned back over on his stomach, and I stood there for a moment studying his contoured back and muscular arms wrapped around two ancient, down feather pillows. I thought to myself, *how in the world were we so lucky to be blessed with such a great kid who is as beautiful outside as he is in?* Then I closed his bedroom door. We never spoke again.

We are all together on this journey of life.
Sharing each other's joys and sorrows.
—Unknown

CHAPTER TWO

FOLLOWING GOD'S PATH

IT SEEMS SO long ago that I came face-to-face with God for the first time. I was 23 years old, married over a year, and not at all ready for the new path laid at my feet. One of three daughters, a twin, we grew up in an upscale suburb of Detroit, Michigan. We had plenty of love and security, golf lessons and country club youth talent shows. Every summer from the time we were 6 yrs. old, we spent six weeks in a mosquito infested area of Canada at a summer camp.

On winter nights, we ice skated on meandering, frozen creeks, which entwined the town of Birmingham. We drank cups of steaming, hot chocolate from thermos bottles that Mom prepared for us. And once, and only once, I lost my lips when I put them on our back gate and they froze to the metal. That was one painful experience I never forgot.

My high school days were filled with club and committee meetings, as well as cheerleading at all the football and basketball games each season from sophomore through senior year. My boyfriend and I either went to the movies, attended sports games, dances or drove through drive-in restaurants ordering a coke while looking for our friends.

At the end of a date, we either made out in the car or on the family room couch after my parents went to bed. Life was very good.

I met my future husband in my freshman year at Michigan State University, and those were the best days of my young life. We each pledged a Greek Sorority/Fraternity organization. He was muscular, tall and blond, handsome and gentle and had been born in Riga, Latvia, on the Baltic Sea. What a refreshing change he was from the majority of boys I had gone out with first semester. We met one Saturday night in the spring, and our relationship continued for the next three years. We married in March, 1962, and lived in married housing at the university while he obtained his graduate degree. I changed majors and received my associate degree in business my senior year while working in the French Department in Foreign Languages.

After the Bay of Pigs regime with President John F. Kennedy and President Castro in Cuba, my husband could see the war with Viet Nam ahead. Since he didn't want to be drafted into the army, he applied to Air Force Officer's Candidate School. He was accepted and we were in a holding pattern waiting for him to be called into the service. At this time in 1963, he also received his Master's Degree in Urban Design and Architecture. Unable to remain in university housing when he graduated, we packed up and moved to Toccoa, Georgia to stay with my parents until he was called into active duty.

My dad began a new job that spring as General Manager of the Wright Manufacturing Co. in Toccoa. He had been with the J. L. Hudson Co. for 33 years, having worked his way up from a scrawny little 16-year-old kid who hoofed his way from Ontario, Canada to downtown Detroit to help support his family of eight. He found a job as a stock boy, and worked his way up to "George Cope-Man of the Year," in the American retail world.

At 55 years of age, Dad was replaced by two MBA Harvard graduates who convinced Corporate that quantity, not quality, would improve the company's bottom line. Dad resigned and left the company after his going-away luncheon with the "proverbial gold watch," in hand.

My husband and I arrived in Toccoa on June 29, 1963. It was a lovely, small town with wooded foothills and a clear blue lake, surrounded by cozy cottages and friendly little family-owned restaurants and customer service shops. The next morning our family went to breakfast together.

After breakfast, Dad and I walked back to our cottage arm-in-arm on a narrow winding road as carloads of vacationers passed by us, gawking as if we were lovers. Along the way, he reminisced about his journey from eighth grade dropout in Canada, to one of the top three executives in this highly successful manufacturing company. He even revealed his yearly salary, which he had never done before. "Wow," I told him, "You are spectacular, Daddy. I love you."

Dad was born with a rheumatic heart, and my sisters and I always shoveled the snow and mowed the lawn so he wouldn't exert excessive stress on his heart. For some reason, he had become obsessed with water skiing and vowed he was going to try it before my sisters and I came to the lake. Each time he brought it up on the phone, we would say, "No way Dad, it's too scary and hard on your heart."

That afternoon, as I ran up to the cottage, Dad walked into the water, put skis on and water skied as if he'd skied all of his life. Coming back down the hill, I saw him and we all stood up and clapped a standing ovation as he made a wide circle, released the rope and let himself down.

The president and vice president of his company encouraged him to rest in the water a moment. Instead, Daddy hauled himself into the boat and laid down. Suddenly, a chair flew, the engine roared, and the boat appeared at our dock. Dad died of a massive heart attack at the age of 55, somewhere between the dock and a doctor's cottage across the lake.

All the years we had watched over him, never allowing him to do overly strenuous activities, and yet, none of us stopped him from getting on those skis. It took a few days to realize that God had placed His hands on our shoulders silently telling us, "You will say nothing.

He is coming with me."

Our Dad died on June 30, 1963. It took two days to make arrangements with an Atlanta funeral home to prepare and transport his body back to Michigan for interment. My twin sister, Nancy, was coming from Chicago with her husband, Erle and their 6-week old baby boy, Mark. Sister, Barb and husband, Bob and their 2-year old daughter, Kathy then had to fly to Michigan. Mom wouldn't bury Dad on July 3 because it was my twin's and my 23rd birthday. Nor would she bury him on the national holiday, July 4th. Dad was buried July 5, 1963.

My Dad's last words to me before I went up to the cottage were, "Honey are you pregnant yet?" My answer was, "No Dad, I think I just got my period. I'll go up and check." And I did have my period. But again, a higher power enabled me to become pregnant in the next 5 days. How strange it was that we had tried to have a baby for the preceding 15 months, and yet, a few nights of comfort with my husband, while we slept on two cots in the basement, was all it took. I overheard someone say at the funeral home, "The Lord giveth, and the Lord taketh away."

On April 10, 1964, our first daughter, Susan Leigh, was born in Walnut Creek, California. Seventeen months later, our second daughter, Sandra Lynn was also born in Walnut Creek. Our little family was just perfect, and we loved this time of our lives with two precious little girls, good friends, velvety foothills surrounding our rent house, the ocean an hour away and the promise of a great future. But nothing too perfect lasts for long.

In 1969, an old college friend called us from Springfield, Illinois to tell my husband that the Department of Conservation, State of Illinois, needed a landscape architect for their state parks. Within two weeks, my husband interviewed and was hired.

We moved from the exuberance and beauty of the Bay Area after Christmas, leaving behind our good friends and a place that always felt like we were on vacation. On our drive to Illinois, our daughters both had a mean case of chickenpox. They slept most of the way in our station wagon, and we ate every meal at a drive-in restaurant to keep from spreading their disease to others.

When we arrived in Springfield, we bought our first home, and borrowing $25,000 made me physically ill in the middle of the night. We adjusted in no time at all. The girls liked their elementary school; we met many good friends, and joined the American Businessmen's Club, which offered all sorts of weekend family activities. I served as Volunteer President of Hope School for the Blind and Mentally Handicapped, joined the Congregational Church, and found life to be very satisfying. At least for a while.

Life is a teacher with the art of relinquishment.
—*Socrates*

CHAPTER THREE

AND THEN THERE WAS MIKE

ON JULY 7, 1973, at 11:07 a.m., we gave birth to an 8-lb. baby boy, Michael John George Falk. We hadn't been able to conceive in eight years, so this baby seemed quite special to all of us. So special, we gave him three names; Michael (in the likeness of God), John and George, after our fathers.

The labor was more intensive with my son. I had shown an intolerance to the drugs given me during my prior labors with the girls, so the doctor's plan was to deliver our baby naturally. After several hours of pushing, suddenly I was ordered to stop pushing. A needle quickly went into my arm to halt the baby's expulsion. The cord was wrapped around Mike's neck.

Our dear baby boy smiled all through infancy, enjoying with great gusto, every food, toy and experience he encountered. He was the easiest toddler, and his mental and physical health seemed to be perfectly in balance. He wasn't timid; he wasn't daring. He had patience, normal learning skills, good coordination and a typical adventurous, inquisitive nature.

Sue and Sandy dressed him up in all sorts of clothes and costumes, and his dad played toddler football on his knees while both of them had Tupperware bowls on their heads.

When recession hit in 1974, particularly in Springfield, the capital city of Illinois, much of my husband's business ground to a halt, and our bank account suddenly dwindled. He came home one afternoon, threw his briefcase on the breakfast table and said, "You better go out and find a job because we're almost out of money."

I opened the newspaper on the table, saw a free seminar in real estate, made a reservation, attended, took state required real estate courses and passed. My retired mother-in-law rented out her house in Michigan, moved to Springfield and took care of our children while I worked.

Mike wasn't born a genius, but he was born with determination and drive. By third grade, one of his teachers felt he had difficulty with perception. We discussed holding him back, since he was born in July and was one of the youngest in his class. Because he was husky for his age and seemed to handle things well, the teachers didn't recommend that he repeat a grade. Mike was sensitive, and they felt it might have a negative effect if they held him back.

In retrospect, would it all have turned out differently had we held him back? Mike was so sweet, innocent and cooperative, he was simply loved by his teachers. We all seemed to have developed a protective attitude with him. I don't remember having that feeling with our girls.

Being a "work mom," I outdid myself to give quality time to Mike. Each morning I would fix Mike a fun breakfast. Most days I served Mickey Mouse pancakes with chocolate chip eyes and nose and a cherry mouth. It made his day.

When he opened his lunch box each day, he would find a special message or a novelty drawing I created on his napkin. They were the hit of the table and he was proud to show them. I volunteered at the school library and cafeteria because it meant a lot to him and gave him extra security. I tried hard to schedule my clients around my family life, while my husband shopped and played sports with him.

In the fourth grade, most of Mike's closest friends were moved into a higher team group, and he was devastated to be left behind. I spoke to his teachers and learned they held him in the same group to separate him from a few of the tactless and sometimes cruel friends who made fun of him because he didn't grasp concepts or conclusions as well or as fast. Neither Mike nor I were very street-smart. I told Mike what the teachers said and he was angry and disappointed.

Mike simply changed overnight. He studied all the time, pushing himself and brought home an all A report card. He was then elevated into the same group as all of his friends. Good or bad, the serious pursuit for perfection became a part of Mike's life. Self-pressure had a strong hold and followed him the rest of his life.

Mike grew up wanting to be a doctor. He took on shoes very hard to fill. His grandfather was a surgeon, his grandmother, an attorney, and his father, an architect. Precision and perfection went hand in hand in each of these fields and seemed inherited.

By the fifth grade, Mike exhibited a keen memory. He readily recited the Preamble, the Declaration of Independence, all the state capitals and most astoundingly, the bones in the body. He declared he definitely wanted to be a physician. But until then, he was going to pursue his greatest love; baseball. And this was his path right up to the end. Over the years, Mike's schedule was demanding. If he wasn't in the classroom, he was on one sports field or another. He was more independent, but still harbored an innocence and a vulnerability quite unlike his adult sisters.

During the 1980's, children began disappearing off the streets. The media reported frightening stories of young children who were kidnapped, drugged and held against their will for pornographic movies. The relaxed and fearless enjoyment of our children took on a new edge. I remember when Mike was 11 years old and he wanted to ride his bike a couple of miles away to hit golf balls on an unused piece of land behind the Plano Recreation Center. I couldn't let him go unless he went with another friend. The isolation of the area was too inviting.

When we were in Colorado Springs at a soccer tournament, we had an afternoon off, and Mike and Billy, his best friend since kindergarten, wanted to go horseback riding. Bill's mom, Sandy, and I took the boys while our husbands watched other soccer teams compete. We had to wait nearly two hours, and by the time it was our turn to ride, Sandy and I talked ourselves out of letting the boys ride because it was raining, and the thought of riding along narrow mountain paths terrified us for our kids.

What were we doing? Were we enabling our kids to be afraid of everything, or was it our inexperience with boys since we both had two girls who were homebodies at that age. When Mike took up golf at age 13, we laughingly told him we wished he would wear a helmet. When he and Bill learned to snow ski, we wanted to wrap them in bubble wrap to keep them from breaking their bones. Was it just me and my friend who felt like this, or did other moms feel their boys were so vulnerable and naïve, they too were cautious and defensive if their boys were mistreated or physically hurt?

In the eighth grade, Mike decided to give up two other sports to play baseball exclusively. "Mom, I'm giving up football and basketball." When I asked why, his response was boyishly serious. "Number 1, I don't want to wrack my knees; Number 2, I'm not mean enough, and number 3, I don't need the glory." His dad and I respected his independent, personal decision.

That summer, having been known for the number of times Mike had received the *Most Valuable Player Award,* he was sought after by several Dallas select baseball teams. He was drafted for his size, batting strength and the fact that he was a left-handed first baseman.

Mike was 14 and his dad and I were growing farther apart. My real estate career was so successful that he decided I was bringing home the bacon instead of just the gravy. He started slacking off from his architectural career and spending many nights drinking with the guys.

He even leased an apartment with his friends for a few months and hung around with girls he called show ponies. He never really wanted the responsibility of taking care of our monthly bills, cooking, cleaning or disciplining our children, and I was growing resentful.

Pulled in so many directions by our personal problems, I couldn't juggle a family and a business by myself. One night, I simply gave it all up to God and begged for help. The next morning, I felt like a new person. We had a family meeting to decide on solutions to end all the weight on my shoulders. And the meeting brought about major changes in our lives.

Our fiercely independent 21-year old daughter, Sue, who had been working and in her own apartment for two years, fractured her ankle when she fell into an open water valve box. She had been off work for over two months, during which I chauffeured her 22 miles to the Texas Unemployment Office and stood in line with all the other unemployed waiting for whatever they could snag from the government. "Sue," I said, "I can't role play with you anymore. You have to find the courage to go out and find a new job!"

Our youngest daughter, Sandy, was a happy-go-lucky college student, spending money like it had an endless supply and having the time of her life in her dorm and sorority. I told her when she returned to school after the holiday, she must get a part-time job. After the girls left the room, I calmly said to my husband, "I'm tired of your negative attitude, finished trying to bolster your self-esteem, sick of all your nights out with the guys, and I expect you to go out and find a decent job somewhere in the United States in the next three months." He had been selling plants and laughing about it. I got up from the table and walked to our bedroom and said, "Yes!" feeling unburdened for the first time in many years.

Within a week, Sue found an interesting job and remained with the same company for 25 years. Sandy sold clothes after class and even got a 20% discount on her clothes. And four months later, my husband found a job in Orlando, Florida. I was sad, but relieved, when he left.

My relief was short-lived.

It was mid-May, 1988, and Mike missed his dad. He started to convince me that he needed to go live with his dad in Florida. His reasoning was sensible, and we both knew it. His dad needed him more because he couldn't cook, wouldn't clean and would be too lonely. He knew his dad would help him practice baseball, they could play golf together, and the independence would be good for him.

I couldn't imagine living without him. I cried for four days after Sue moved to an apartment. In the end, Mike went to Florida. Silly as it seemed, I collected very cute family craft dolls and caught myself smiling at them after I was living totally alone. Actually, it was the first time I had ever lived alone in my entire life, having had a twin, roommate, spouse or child.

Sandy graduated from college in the field of advertising. She found two part-time jobs in her field and raced from Plano down to Dallas. With no benefits, she applied for a job with American Airlines and a week later was accepted. I flew every other weekend to be with Mike and his dad because of all of our family passes. Mike was a walk-on at Winter Park High School and he nabbed first base. The team was good and they ended up taking regional playoffs. He loved it there playing golf, practicing baseball every day and traveling all over the state.

Mike and his dad were like two proud bachelors. Each time I visited, the apartment was shining. Hills did the laundry, Mike the cooking, and they shared the cleaning. They seemed to share a great closeness, and although I missed him so much, I thought this arrangement was the best thing for him.

Mike was really growing up and becoming very responsible. He continually earned A's in school in spite of every day of baseball practice. Each time they took me back to the airport to leave, I cried, but I knew in my heart that he was doing exactly what he wanted to do. We were together every Thanksgiving, Christmas, New Years, spring break and second half of the summer when Florida baseball ended.

His dad and I came to the mutual decision to get divorced when

Mike was a junior in high school. We wrote our own expectations and presented them to our joint attorney. Our divorce was quiet, amicable and swift. It was actually so effortless, the attorney forgot to bill us. People who went through hell getting a divorce don't believe us when we tell them ours was free.

I continued to fly down during the remainder of Mike's junior and senior year. The guys each had a bedroom upstairs, and I slept in the living room. We were friends. It never felt awkward. Even when Hill's girlfriend came to watch Mike play, we all sat together. Mike seemed to find it amusing.

Being well known for their regional win in his senior year, he and several guys on his team were invited to play for the Houston Astro Scouts Team in Orlando. That was the best hands-on experience Mike ever encountered. As a result, he was offered scholarships at several Southeast colleges. Mike, his dad and his coach decided the best experience he could get was to play locally at a baseball-rich junior college. He would get the value of continuous playing time rather than sit on second string at one of the large Georgia or Florida baseball teams.

Mike was playing ball on a scholarship at Valencia Junior College, staying in a team financed apartment. Four guys shared a two-bedroom, two bath unit, and he was excited to be on his own for the first time. His roommate was a senior, and they were both very disciplined and worked hard for good grades.

The other two guys lived it up, trying to stay in school while making history with the nightly beer consumption and number of nightly gal pals. Mike was amazed at their living habits and recklessness. I kind of felt it was a good learning experience for him to see how others lived. He had always been naïve and sheltered in the sterile environment in which he grew up.

During the summer of 1992, the coach at Huntingdon College in Montgomery, Alabama contacted Mike when he had an open position for a first baseman. He was pumped and saw this as a great opportunity to make something of himself since the school had a good baseball reputation, having produced some outstanding players in the past. It was a Methodist school, and it seemed to be exactly right for him.

While Mike was playing on his summer league team in Florida, I became engaged to Rod, whom I had met shortly after my divorce in the spring of 1989. We were friends first, because we had both been married over twenty-five years and weren't sure we were ready to try it again. So, for three years we dated. When it became apparent that our relationship was heading for permanency, we worked hard on all of our differences to be sure we were compatible.

I loved Rod's sense of responsibility. His quick, dry humor won me over in no time at all. He called me a woman of the world, and always wondered what I would want with a country boy from Paducah. His beautiful smile, his kindness and thoughtfulness, and his romantic ways of showing affection did it for me.

Summer ball ended mid-July, and Mike spent the remainder of the summer with me. Our threesome worked well together. Rod left at night because he didn't want Mike to feel uncomfortable, but also to go home to his son and daughter who were high school students living with their dad ever since their mom left them for another man in 1987.

Fall of 1992 was a happy time for Mike. He played great ball traveling all over Alabama and bordering states. He developed great friendships with his new teammates and enjoyed the attention of many young girls who found his genuine niceness, dimpled smile and shy, innocent ways very appealing. His 6'2" athletic body and compelling good looks weren't missed either.

Modest and unassuming, he was shocked with all the attention from girls. He had always been such a serious student and driven athlete, he never seemed to have had time for girls. Now that he was really on his own, he found new pleasure in his freedom.

Rod and I were married the day after Christmas, 1992, and our six grown children were our attendants. We hosted a fun reception for friends and family and honeymooned in New Orleans for four days, returning to our new home for a quiet New Year's Eve celebration with our friends. All of our children had places to go and we felt blessed to have a combined family. Mike fell in love for the first time in his life, and he fell hard. We heard about it almost every night. From the south, Leslie was a lovely all-American, long haired beauty with a 4.0 grade point average through high school and now in her first year of college. She also had a part-time modeling job in Mobile, AL. Her goal was to qualify for the Astronaut Program after college.

They became serious in his junior year, but not without their share of problems. He wasn't sure he could trust her completely, and she wasn't thrilled with the idea of him spending so much time on the field or traveling to away games. Inexperienced, he hadn't a clue about how to handle her feelings.

Mike was much taller and almost two years older than Leslie. He watched over her protectively and called her his little girl. He loved this new feeling and learned how to unwind at parties. He even called me saying he was completely shocked at how his life had changed so much. He asked if he had been a nerd in high school when he was always running to be on time for class and so diligent with his homework.

His teammates told Mike that his girlfriend was messing with his head. His female friends warned him against Leslie, but he felt they might just be jealous. His 3.6 GPA slipped, and although that bothered him, he spent every minute with her when he wasn't on the ball field or studying.

In the spring of 1994, Mike surprisingly told his coach that everybody was fed up with his belittling and sarcasm. In Mike's eyes, the coach lacked respect for him and most of the guys on his team except for those he called "The Kiss-ups." With Leslie's encouragement, Mike quit the team.

Being away from baseball for over a week, Mike regretted his decision greatly. He apologized to his coach and asked to be put back on the team. The coach told him indifferently that he would put it to a vote among the team. The team voted him back in except for the first baseman who had replaced him. It didn't matter anyway because the coach benched him the rest of the season.

Years before this, Mike's summer coach in the eighth grade (a past pro baseball player) saw so much promise in Mike he suggested that he focus strictly on baseball. When Mike didn't sign up for the football team that fall, the football coach, who was also a baseball coach, refused to let him play the first six games. Dads of teammates knew how good Mike played and intimidated the coach into putting Mike back on the field, and he performed exceptionally well, as always. That was the year we learned that school coaches differed greatly from recreational team coaches, and politics played heavily on sports fields.

Mike returned home mid-May of his junior year. Five months earlier he had applied to transfer to the University of Texas, Texas A & M and North Texas State for scholastic and sports purposes. He had confidence in his grades, but was uncertain if he would lose some credits in the transfer. He was also home too late to sign up for recreational baseball and was bummed about it.

At the end of May, 1994, Mike was alarmed that he hadn't heard back from any of the three schools he applied to. He called each of their registrar's offices only to learn that his first-year transcripts from Valencia College had not been received so his applications hadn't been processed. He knew that Huntingdon had all of his transcripts and assumed they would all be sent together. He missed the small print saying that original transcripts must be sent from each school attended.

It was now July and even though Valencia agreed to quickly send his freshman year transcript to each of the schools, he also found out from Huntingdon's records office that his final semester's transcript had not been forwarded because his coach had not released Mike's scholarship money. Calls to the coach went unanswered. Finally, after two weeks, we went to the top to get the money released and transcript sent. The power within a coach reared its ugly head for the third time in this boy's greatly admired and respected life.

While Mike anguished over all the delays, he talked to counselors at the schools to find out if all of his credits would transfer. Without complete transcripts, they were unable to assure him. He worried whether he would be a senior, junior or even a sophomore again. To add to his pressures, Leslie called to say she wanted to transfer to Texas as well. He then became concerned that he couldn't keep up in his pre-med classes, get back into baseball and keep her happy all at the same time.

Mike was beside himself. Every day, twice a day, sometimes four times a day we walked around the block talking things through. I was surprised that he was so fearful and dismayed over all of his decisions. I gave him all the assurance I could. I gave him a book about positive thinking and reminded him daily to trust in God to give him direction and to put it in his hands.

While his whole life was on hold, minute by minute, Mike decided to enroll in Collin County Community College in Plano to pick up extra credits just in case. He took physiology, kinesiology and a computer class. I hoped it would take his mind off of his problems.

Within a few weeks he was exhausted and burned out. He stopped attending and formed a lawn mowing service with Bill and did internship at the hospital for valuable resume experience. Was he escaping his anguish by working twelve-hour days?

It became obvious that Mike was letting every little thing bother him to excess; transporting their lawn mowers, billing, weather delays, etc. This was a side of Mike our family had never seen. We felt that he just had too much on his mind and having had a past of total discipline and structure in school and sports, we considered these difficulties would recede as soon as he received his acceptances.

Mike turned 21 years-old on July 7, and he and four friends went out to celebrate. Even though Mike wasn't much of a drinker, we were surprised that he was home before midnight. The girls and I wondered why it didn't seem like such a big deal to be 21, but we had often thought of him as an old soul; an appreciator of Frank Sinatra; a loyal watcher of Miss America with me! Late in July, two of Mike's buddies from Alabama arrived for a week of golf. He seemed to enjoy their visit, but also seemed somewhat quieter than usual. After the boys left, he resumed his extreme unsettled confusion about his uncertain future. And then came Leslie.

Leslie flew in from Alabama to spend a week with Mike. He wasn't sure which of the three universities he would most likely attend, so he and Leslie drove down to College Station, TX. to check out the junior college they could attend until they could start A & M. or Univ. of Texas.

At the end of her stay, Leslie decided she would come down permanently the end of August, live with Sandy, Mike's sister in her apartment in Dallas since Sandy was flying a lot with American Airlines. Her parents really liked Mike and had confidence in his ability to handle their situation in a grown up, safe way. The only requirement her parents had was that she attend classes in the day and work at night.

Mike and Bill dissolved their lawn service, and he flew to Florida to visit his dad before flying to Mobile to gather Leslie and her belongings and drive her car to Texas. The day after they arrived here they encountered a setback.

Mike had already signed up for his pre-med classes earlier at the Collin County Community College in Plano and had reminded Leslie to select her required courses electronically from the catalog they picked up. Leslie decided to wait until she got here and could read the course descriptions more closely. Too late! Her courses were totally filled at all three CCCC locations.

Nothing went right for them. They sat at the house for days trying to come up with another organized plan for the brief months ahead before the January semester began. Already homesick by now, Leslie became restless and argumentative. Mike became totally exasperated because he somehow felt responsible for her coming to Texas in the first place. Something un-namable was happening. After several tense confrontations, both Mike and Leslie seemed to lighten up. She decided to return home, work until January, return to Texas and enter Texas A

& M together. The next day, her dad flew in and drove Leslie and her car back to Alabama. Mike seemed relieved, or so I thought.

Mike and I had spent the entire summer hashing and rehashing his thoughts, his fears, his confusion and his inability to make anything move ahead any faster. I loved him so much I spent hours listening, advising, encouraging and assuring him that I could understand his helplessness, but that we would support him and get him through it all. How little I really knew. How wrong I was. How unprepared I was for what was soon to happen.

Its September, 1994, and it seemed as if Mike was less apprehensive. He enrolled back into classes and was spending a lot of time studying in his room. We were upstairs in our office next to his bedroom, and we would talk back and forth as he studied.

Mike's friends had now left for college. He didn't seem to be exercising as much. Wait a minute! Was he exercising at all? "Are you still going to the gym?" I asked. "No, not really, it's not much fun going alone, but I'll still be running around here on the bike trail." Just enough to placate me, it occurs to me now. We were so swamped in our real estate business at that time, I'm sure we missed so much more.

Looking back now, Mike seemed to be so tired all of the time. I attributed it to boredom and the constant never having answers to all of his quandaries. He called Bill and decided to go down to A & M to really look the school over to make sure that was the decision he would make

The day he left for College Station, TX. he looked so sharp I took a picture of him at his car. He turned before getting behind the wheel, looked up at me where I was standing at the front door, and said, "I hope they don't find me dead on the side of the road!" I froze. "Why would you say something so awful?" No answer. "Are you just being dramatic?" Smile, smile, "Yeah Mom." And off he went for the weekend.

Mike drove in from College Station on Sunday, and Rod and Sandy and I were on the patio having a drink and enjoying the first hint of fall. It was about 5:00 p.m. and Mike came out and collapsed on a lawn chair, saying what a rough trip it was. He looked so exhausted and unhealthy. Of course, as usual, he had an easy answer. "We had a blast partying. I drank too much and hardly had any sleep," he groaned. And as always, we believed whatever he said. Why wouldn't we? He was a kid too good to be true. He never made waves, and we never had occasion to argue. Unreal.

The next week was Labor Day. Sue and Mickey were going to Lake Texoma with their jet skis and asked Mike to go with them. He said he had way too much studying to do. We didn't make any plans and just hung around the house for the weekend.

Suddenly Mike had the thought that maybe he should sign up for the Air Force or Navy. He called a good friend from school that was serving in the military. Jamie discouraged him from even thinking about it. Mike's Uncle Bob, who served in Viet Nam and flew planes, also strongly discouraged him from such a decision in his senior year. Sandy's boyfriend, Jim was a pilot for American Airlines and encouraged him to complete school, get a degree and then decide what he wanted to do. We never said a word because we wanted Mike to make his own decisions. Ours would have been so negative anyway.

I suggested that maybe he should think about being a coach since he had such respect and it would take off the pressure of 8 years of medical studies. I suggested that maybe he could go to see his grandmother in Michigan and visit friends at other colleges during that three-month period before the winter semester started. He said he would give it some thought.

Mike ate dinner with Sandy Labor Day. We ate at a friend's house. She had been a social worker after college and I brought up the subject of Mike's dilemmas and apprehensions. She thought Mike might be depressed.

When we arrived home after dinner, I ran to Mike's room and announced that I knew what his problem was. "You're depressed," I said. "That's what's the matter." Thinking of that moron remark, as if the word depressed gave the problem a name and therefore, solved it, makes me sick to this day. In 1994, the world of depression, anxiety, suicide was hardly a blip on the surface of life. Mental health was greatly ignored, hush hushed and until 1999, remained under the rug.

The word, "depression," meant little to me because it wasn't a part of our life. It was just a word I'd heard but never dealt with. It was like, "Ok, now we know what's wrong-why you have been worrying so much. My word for it had been "worrywart." Believe me, I was a hands-on-mom with intelligence, instinct, eyes out for safety and a mother lion in care and love.

The next day, Tuesday, Mike was a completely different person. His whole face lit up with gentleness—a wonderful smile sought our approval, and of course, I was thrilled. "My God, you look like a different person," I gasped, "Have you truly seen that this is just a temporary setback and it's all going to work out ok?" "Yeah mom. It's only 4 months .... that's not so long to wait to get back into school." Oh, dear God, if only I had known the truth of what this placid reaction indicated.

Thursday night, September 15, I cooked Mike his favorite meal; chicken and rice. After dinner, he jumped up and started clearing the table. "You don't have to do that, sit down." He grinned back and said, "It's the least I can do." Rod put his arm around him and said, "She's sure lucky she's got two such great guys, isn't she?" Mike beamed and agreed. What else was new?

Friday, September 16, was quite a wild day for us. It had been an unbelievable month putting eleven sales together. As Rod and I toiled long hours in our office upstairs, Mike stayed in his room most of the day studying. Around 4:00 p.m. we decided to go to the movies to get away from the stress for a couple of hours. We asked Mike to come with us, but he said he was going to dinner with Bill and his family

We got back from the movies about 6:00 p.m. and found Mike still in his room. Bill had never called. I was so not happy. Too many times they had not connected as planned. So, we went downstairs and ate the tuna fish sandwiches Mike had made for our dinner.

Later that night, Bill came over and he and Mike played Chinese Checkers while Rod and I watched television. Mike was dressed in a tee shirt and khaki shorts and looked pale.

We were so tired, we said good night and went to bed at 10 p.m. I didn't kiss Mike as I normally would have because he seemed preoccupied with the game. Rod awoke shortly before midnight when Bill was on his way out.

They had been watching something on television and laughing. I never knew what they were laughing about. Never would I have dreamed that they would not laugh together again in their lifetime.

"There is a certain sadness when it is all over. The compelling purpose all the life of a baseball player is suddenly gone when the game is over. There is nowhere else to go...."

—*Mickey Mantle*

An angel, an angel, sat on his shoulder,
watching him smile all day.
An angel, an angel, sat on his shoulder
ready to take him away.
For God loaned him to us, he simply came through us
and now he's found a new way.
An angel, an angel, now sits on my shoulder.
Keeping me safe every day.
An angel, an angel, now sits on my shoulder.
Helping me find a new way…

I Love You
—Mom

CHAPTER FOUR

STANDING STILL

Saturday, September 17, 1994

AFTER A GREAT day of fishing up at Lake Texoma, we were a mile from home and had just passed the Plano Recreation Center. "My God, Rodney, how in the world are Ashley Estelle's parents surviving?" Ashley had been abducted the year before, right off of the soccer fields where a huge tournament was being held. A very sick person snatched her, put her in his car, drove to a quiet gravel road, killed her and threw her out on the side of the road. It was exactly 5:18 p.m.

As I ran through the house looking for Mike to show him the gigantic bass I had caught, I was surprised that he and Bill weren't watching the football game in our family room as I had expected. The television in Mike's room was airing a soccer game, but he wasn't watching it. He wasn't in his bathroom. "Mike, where are you?"

I knew he was there. I'd seen his car parked in front when we came around the corner. Maybe he and Bill ran out for something to eat. I went into our bedroom and put my things down. Puzzled, as I had passed our bathroom, I saw a toy gun on the floor of the bathroom. As I went back to the bathroom and walked farther into the room, I thought, *"How in the world would a toy gun get here?* I picked up the gun. **OH JESUS… OH JESUS……OH JESUS….. OH JESUS… OH JESUS… OH MY GOD… IT'S SO HEAVY… OH MY GOD, IT'S REAL.**

Shocked, I threw it and as I did, I looked up, and there in our whirlpool tub, was my son, Mike. Clad in a tee shirt and shorts, reclined in the sun streaming in the bath window, his eyes were closed and he had a look of peace on his face. The sudden realization of his color and stillness sent me over the EDGE!!!!!!

A wild, terrified scream sounded. It was ME! The agonizing scream came from ME! **OH MY GOD. MY SON. THAT'S MY SON. MY SON IS DEAD. NO GOD NO. NO!** I was completely out of my mind screaming for my husband to come in from the garage. I tumbled halfway down the stairway, running from the image, and I collapsed on the landing. Urine gushed down my legs.

My husband, Rod shot by me two steps at a time, screaming, "Is there someone up there?" In a strangled sob, I moaned, "Someone killed Mike. Oh God, oh God, oh God, oh God." 911…Rod was frantically trying to explain. I was wailing like a mad woman to hurry, get help. All the questions—All the lost time. *"Help ME…OH GOD…HELP ME."* One minute I was leaping around, babbling out of control, like a lunatic. The next minute I was mute and frozen in place, downstairs on the slanting cushions of the cold, cream colored couch. How did I get there?

Several police officers drifted in and out of the family room. Out of nowhere, a chaplain sat down beside me. He patted my hand and asked me some dumb questions. I tried to respond but I couldn't think. "So, you think someone came in and killed your son this afternoon?" he asked. I murmured, "Everyone loved Mike, no one would hurt him. It must have been a burglar."

He gently took my hand, and I remember that he said so compassionately, "But do you really think someone would kill your son in the bathtub?" I asked him what he was trying to say.

"Would Mike have done this to himself?" Somewhere in the way-far-back of my jumbled mind, I thought, *well….it would be just like Mike to keep from making a mess…….*

Just as mysteriously as the chaplain appeared, he disappeared. And there I sat, mouth desert-dry, barely able to breath, shivering with still damp hair, and a partially wet bathing suit. The air-conditioned room was freezing, and I couldn't find the words to say I was cold. I was so thirsty, but words failed me when I needed to ask for something to drink.

Our friends, Jarry and Donna, had come from their home a few blocks away, and they sat looking at me, utterly speechless. Neighbors drifted in. I was so bewildered; I couldn't communicate at all.

"Where are my children? Oh God, do my girls know? Does Mike's dad, oh no Mike's grandmother, do they know? Dear God this will kill them. Where are my girls?" I wailed.

Word had somehow spread like fire, from friend to friend, and there seemed to be so many people standing and milling around, their eyes fastened on mine, brimming with tears of sorrow. Every time I looked up at them from my seat on the slippery couch, I was reminded that something unbelievably impossible had happened.

I slipped out of the heaviest fog long enough to plead, "Please somebody, I need a diet coke. Could I have someone's cigarette? I know I quit but I need one now. A pill? What kind of pill? No, I don't want a pill! I'm so cold. Why am I so cold?" I whined. "Eat? Eat? How can I eat? I can't eat! I can't live. I don't even want to live."

I don't know how long I just sat in that one place staring with dead eyes. I was in such a peculiar state of being. My mind floated with numbness, too weak and confused to go forward. It just felt safer to stay put in this bewildering place of white, quiet nothingness.

Suddenly, there was Sue. Someone was wrestling with her to keep her from going upstairs. "That's not Mike up there," she screamed, "Let me go, let go of me, dammit! I've got to get to Mike. It's not Mike up there."

There were yellow crime scene ribbons draped across the stairs, so I heard. And evidently, the police wouldn't let anyone go up while they do whatever it is that police do in matters such as this.

I finally got up off the couch and went to my Sue. "Sue, it's Mike. I saw him. It's true." "No Mom," she moaned, "it's not Mike. Are you crazy? Mike wouldn't do this!" It took several seconds to sink in. She doubled over and collapsed, sobbing. My heart went out to her as I held her, but I really couldn't feel her pain. I was too numb with my own.

And then Sandy anxiously rushed into the room, having been told by Sue's husband, Mickey, on the drive over, that Mike had been hurt. Her denial of her brother's condition convinced her that as soon as she could get to him, she would be able to do something about it. She was totally shocked to arrive amidst police cars, fire engine and ambulance. She fell down when Sue confirmed that Mike was dead. They wept uncontrollably together, as I knelt down in a stupor and looked on.

I wondered a couple of times why Rod wasn't seated beside me. Each time I saw him he was rushing back and forth, keeping very busy. I wasn't sure I needed him, I just wondered why he was so distracted. I later learned that he had called everyone in our family, good friends of ours and Mike's and made arrangements for our minister to come. He also handled the funeral home arrangements and everything else imaginable that must be done under these circumstances.

How in the world would we ever have been able to make it without him? And this was just the beginning of the way he took charge and literally kept me making baby steps toward living.

When I turned around on the couch and looked outside, it was dark. How had it become dark? I went to the bathroom, and someone was able to get upstairs and get me a sweatshirt and pants to stop me from shaking.

By now, it must have been 8 or 9:00 p.m. Rod's daughter, Jill and son, Bret had arrived. Sandy's fiancée, Jim, was there. Sue's husband Mickey was utterly distraught. Mike was like a brother to him since he had started dating Sue in 1985.

Everything seemed to be moving in slow motion. Was everyone there in shock? Why were so many people standing in small groups everywhere, barely speaking and always turning around to stare at me? I kept thinking, my God, I can't grasp why all of these people are floating in circles helplessly. This is scaring me. Am I drugged? What exactly happened upstairs? All I could do was sit, mummified, on the couch, not having wits enough to console the crowd.

Suddenly, my friend, Nancy, who had recently lost her dad in an automobile accident, flew at me, wild-eyed, from out of nowhere. She grabbed me and shook me in hysterics. All we could do next was hold each other, and as mothers, sob in total disbelief. "Of all the kids in the world, Mike would be the last one anyone would ever dream of killing himself," she cried. If it happened to Mike, it could happen to any of our friend's kids. And everyone was probably as paralyzed by this as we were.

I heard someone say that the ambulance left with Mike, and the police had finished their business, conferring with Rod before they left. Some period of time later, Rod came downstairs with a paper in his hand. He quietly told us that the police had not found a final letter written by Mike. Inadvertently, Rod found it himself. Mike's anatomy book, which lay open to a page showing the human heart, was next to his spiral notebook. Rod found Mike's handwritten letter near the back of the notebook. Now he took my hand in his and directed our family into a private circle.

The reality hit me right there. MIKE TOOK HIS OWN LIFE.............................As Rod read the letter, I knew that Mike must have been trying, in his practical way, to explain himself with simplicity and sincerity. He talked about the few goals he set for himself in being a good father and a major-league baseball player. He said he made mistakes in choices of schools and coaches, and that he never seemed to be in the right place at the right time. He felt he found himself to be without much personality toward the end of his life, and he couldn't enjoy life as it was meant to be enjoyed. He knew he had always put too much pressure on himself when instances didn't demand that pressure, but that he couldn't help it

Mike wrote that he no longer had direction or statement of purpose. He said he had always thought he could live his life as long as he was happy, but that he could no longer see that as being possible. He didn't want us to blame his girlfriend. He said that perhaps the circumstances which led to their separation until January might have been meant to be.

He let us know that he hoped he would see us after we had all lived happy and successful lives, and that he could not have asked for a more loving and caring family than what he had. He signed the letter with his full given name.

We all just looked at each other and seemed to say, in unison, "This is not Mike! This is not the Mike we knew.!" The way he saw himself was all wrong. Wishing us all the success we deserved. We all looked at each other with total skepticism. This was not Mike; this is a boy we didn't even recognize. It left us completely hollow. It screamed *MISTAKE....... MISTAKE.... A DEAD WRONG MISTAKE...........*

Although this was not our Mike, we now understood, whether in his right mind or not, Mike ended the pain evidently raging within him. Pain we had failed to recognize; pain we never saw nor heard. How long had this part of Mike been unknown to all of us who loved him so much for 21 years? He never cried, he showed no anger; he smiled so much, and to think we only knew that he was worrying about things that didn't warrant that much worry! *GOD ALMIGHTY...* where were my instincts? Why wouldn't he tell me he was worried about himself.

Why didn't he say, "I'm going nuts, Mom, maybe we should go to a shrink!" I collapsed back on the couch and seemed again engulfed in a distancing stillness. Was this the shock protection place? Time got away from me while I was completely encapsulated in what seemed like a soft cocoon. Eventually, I noticed people had left. Where had I been?

My saddened friends told me I should go to bed. I needed sleep they said. Sleeping pills appeared out of nowhere; prescribed by someone; delivered at some time while I was in another world. I took the offered pill, hoping it would put me out of ever waking up.

Everyone was gone. I was faced with an exhaustive urge to sleep. Fear consumed me. I could not go upstairs and face the room where Mike had taken his life. I was too afraid to close my eyes for fear I would see the vision of my dead son. I was suddenly petrified that I could lose my daughters just as quickly as I lost my son.

Rod already felt I wouldn't go upstairs so he had help bringing down a queen mattress from one of the beds and had covered it with sheets for us. He held me as I cried exhaustively. I had practically lost my voice by then, and the effort of making even the slightest sound took so much energy. I awoke hourly, only to the horror that Mike was gone. *Oh God, Mike is gone.* I heard my own strange moans and wails until again, I slept for another brief period.

September 18, 1994

My son died yesterday. I can't get away from it. The pain is killing me. ***I Can't DO THIS!! HELP ME...GOD HELP ME***

Around 6:00 a.m., Rod led me upstairs to take a shower. I showered with my eyes closed, so that I wouldn't have to see the bathtub. He picked out my clothes, helped me dress and I went downstairs to sit and think about how I could make it all be different. The telephone rang by 7:00 a.m. Pots of coffee were brewed and my friends, Donna and Joyce, handled things in the kitchen as if they had been permanently employed there for years.

It seemed so odd to me to have someone taking charge of my kitchen, but I just sort of shrugged, and sat down to get to my task of fantasizing the nightmare away. The day began in utter despondency. I was so irritated at the excessive noise and action surrounding me, because I just couldn't seem to concentrate on my task. Phones rang endlessly. Food arrived as if a catered party was in the making.

Friends who weren't at our home last night were showing up to hold me, cry with me, urge me to eat, rest, keep my faith, take care of myself. What could I say? What they said I needed was 360 degrees from what I knew I needed to do to bring Mike back to us. Sue and Sandy arrived, and we stared pitifully at one another with no words. We were so shell-shocked; we were virtually speechless.

The constant shrill ring of telephones was the only reminder I had of life outside my secret place of white stillness. Our friends were writing down airline schedules, hotel reservations, availability of neighbor's refrigerators and freezers to house the incoming food donations. It all seemed just too tiring and too confusing to concentrate. So again, I retreated into my private struggle to turn everything that had happened completely around so I could be just fine again. In the midst of it all, I gasped when I heard that my first husband of 27 years, our children's dad and his girlfriend were coming up the walk after arriving from Florida. I met them in the foyer with our daughters, and all the world seemed to stand still for a few minutes.

Sobbing, we clung together in a circle to hang on to each other tightly, as if to keep one another from drowning. Our friends stood by and helplessly watched our family's overwhelming anguish. Privacy was non-existent. It didn't matter.

During the day, airport runs brought each of my sisters. My twin sister, Nancy arrived from Aspen, Colorado, and my older sister, Barb, and her husband, Bob arrived from Fairfax, Virginia. It seemed odd to me that their presence failed to bring me any comfort. It wasn't the usual joyous occasion to see one another again. Was there no one who could help me? Couldn't someone just explain all of this, and make me understand how Mike could actually be gone, and why he would ever think to end his life and destroy ours?

Leslie and her parents arrived from Mobile, Al. No one could speak. We hugged. Leslie kept looking down. Did she think I blamed her? Did she know something we didn't? Oh GOD.

Our minister, Harvey and his wife Ruth came to the house and brought homemade chicken noodle soup, which turned out to be the only food I could go near for the next four or five days. (It is also the very thing I take to others who have lost a loved one, for I know that it plays a mighty role in helping the distraught to keep going).

Harvey brought Rod and me together with our children's dad to make decisions regarding the service. Being the musician in our family, I knew in an instant, the type of music Mike would have picked, had he been there for the occasion. I chose *On the Wings of Love* and *I Don't Have the Heart*, songs sung by James Ingram, an artist whom Mike and I both loved. We did not want heavy, doom-filled organ music or lectures. We wanted a tribute to a boy we all loved so much, and who must have had a brain chemical imbalance for him to do something so out of character and so devastating, not only to himself and our family, but to his friends and others who knew and cared about him.

Rod made a call to his office at the Dallas Independent School District Administration building. As happens sometimes, call it fate, he talked to just the right person when he asked for a particular type of singer, and Loretta knew just the right person for the job. And just the perfect person knew a perfect pianist to accompany him and he happened to be available for the funeral services. Arrangements were made quickly-or maybe I was out of touch about time.

All day long, platters of meat, casseroles, vegetables, salads, desserts, bags of plastic ware and paper goods arrived. The system was master planned. My tireless friends, Donna, Joyce and Charlie checked in the dishes with an accurate record of everything. They arranged the food on the dining room table, or stowed it away for the next shift. They recorded each and every phone call, visitor, and floral arrangements to our home or the church.

People from all over the country, who had mysteriously found out about the loss of our son, called to extend their sympathy or inform us they were flying or driving in. Mike's friends called, crying and swearing. I was stupefied by it all. As the first full day of the rest of my life went on,

I was either sobbing or quiet and dream-like. Sips of soup and sleeping pills enabled me to drift listlessly from Sunday to Monday.

Monday, September 19, 1994

MIKE IS GONE. REALLY GONE. NEVER COMING BACK

Mike's dear, darling paternal grandmother, Mimi, an iron horse of eighty some odd years, a lady who had survived two wars unscathed, arrived visibly shaken, and obviously devastated. Mimi had become my mom after my own mother died four years previously. The thought of my mom seeing Mike arrive in heaven briefly touched on my mind at one point.

Sue, Sandy and Leslie chose the clothes Mike would wear for the viewing and burial. They also picked items they wanted to place near his heart before he was laid to rest. Then we picked his casket. God knows what a difficult task this was. Our last required decision was to pick out a plot Mike would be buried in and pen an inscription for his marker.

Hillar, Rod, Mimi, Sue, Sandy, Leslie, and I joined the representative from Restland Cemetery in Dallas for a tour of the various sections of vacant ground available for purchase. What an unusual education. One section featured a restful water pond, complete with swans. Another area had a garden and a babbling brook. Others were heavy with trees. Each area that had more to offer became pricier as we went along.

We easily settled on a peaceful spot overlooking the tiny cemetery chapel to the west and the swan pond to the south. The plot was surrounded by six tall trees, which without much effort, boldly suggested the six members of our family, including Mimi.

Funny how important trees became when laying our beloved child to rest. I insisted he have that protection of shade. How insignificant money seemed at the time. Buying the perfect place to bury our child seemed to be priceless. Completing the horrendous decisions demanded of us, we drove home to dress for the viewing. I couldn't believe how anxious I was to see Mike again. How insane was I? When we arrived at the funeral home, the girls and I went in alone first. Mike looked very good, considering. Considering what? Considering he was dead? He looked peaceful and actually had a slight smile, sort of.

His hair was all wrong. We told the hovering beautician, and she quickly changed it to the way he was wearing it when he was last alive. OH, MY GOD. Something was missing. I kept looking for what it was. Then it hit me! Where had Mike's dimples gone? He didn't look right without them. When I was alone, after the girls had walked away in tears, I poked at his cheeks repeatedly. I suddenly realized it was the very last thing I would ever be able to do for my son again.

After the viewing, friends and family returned to our home. It was actually an uplifting evening. People were being themselves again. The Dallas Cowboys were playing on Monday Night Football, and people were mindlessly enjoying themselves. I was kept occupied, and felt very close to all of those around me. I had a couple of drinks that night, and actually relaxed and slept for six uninterrupted hours.

Tuesday, September 20, 1994

BURIAL TODAY. NOT REAL. JUST NOT REAL GOD.

We were amazed to see hundreds of cars at the cemetery. People were lined up in the hall waiting to view our son. People we hadn't seen in years were there for us. So overwhelming. When the line had gone through to say goodbye to Mike, our family was ushered into the viewing room for individual private moments with him. I turned to wave to a friend, and suddenly I saw Mike's entire baseball team coming down the hall, having traveled all night from Montgomery, Alabama to see their friend, their first baseman, for the last time.

Thirty stalwart, but fragile young men silently lined up to say goodbye. Along with the guys came five or six of Mike's closest female friends. Parents stood by looking on, privately thanking God it wasn't their child in the casket. The shocking appearance of so many sad young people made mothers cry and dads outwardly stiff and uncomfortable.

I knew several of Mike's closest friends on the team and hugged them as they introduced me to the others in line. The coach must have planned beforehand that this would be a learning experience for each of the boys for the rest of their lives. Why did our son have to be the lesson plan?

After the team went through, Hillar, Mimi and the girls and Leslie went to see Mike for the last time. When it was my turn and I realized that I would never, ever see my son again, I was just paralyzed. I couldn't leave his side. I couldn't make myself move away. I needed to keep him warm, he was so cold. How in the hell was I supposed to just leave him alone forever? Our lives were now truly shattered.

The funeral director led me away to keep the schedule moving. After the closed casket was situated at the front of the sanctuary and the flowers skillfully arranged, we were brought over in a group to walk down the center aisle to the front pews.

We moved unsteadily down, aware of the hundreds of friends, young and old, compelled to be present at this most supportive time. The anguish of people grieving over the death of a young person seemed to be magnified.

The powerful sense of horror demanded the comfort of words and prayers and the closeness of touch. I recognized an awesome strength and that allowed me to get through Harvey's meaningful service with a bravery I thought I had forever lost.

The service was flawless, as if it had been rehearsed several times. Mike would have appreciated its perfection. Mike's Uncle Bob told heartwarming stories about Mike. Sue's husband, Matt, brought tears to the eyes of many when he spoke of his admiration and love for his young brother-in-law who was more like a brother. Look at all those so hurt by Mike's act.

Pastor Anderson delivered a moving sermon with an astounding illustration that brought understanding and comfort to the mourners. Strong lyrics of love and forgiveness in the beautiful songs we chose were sung by an African American man who had won a spot on Star Search recently, accompanied by a talented pianist. The powerful depth and quality of the songs touched the audience as much as Mike and I had always been touched by the songs we loved.

Prior to the service when Sue said goodbye to Mike, she had silently asked him to give her a sign that he was with us in spirit. Just when the singer ended his first song, for no apparent reason, a small lacy leaf detached itself from Mimi's casket spray and slowly floated down upon the carpet. Sue, Sandy, Mimi and Leslie all saw it happen. They looked at each other, got my attention, and with certainty whispered in unison, "Mike is here."

While I sat there staring at the casket, I thought of the dear treasures the girls picked to lay with Mike. Leslie had placed the heavy gold chain necklace she had given him for his 21st birthday around his neck. His dad placed by his side, his SAE fraternity sweat shirt at Michigan State University and his #25 baseball shirt. The girls put in family pictures, his baseball and bat.

There couldn't have been a more beautiful day for Mike's interment. It was sunny and a crisp 70-degree temperature range. Sandy's boyfriend, Jim had thoughtfully purchased dozens of elegant, white, long-stemmed roses to be placed on the casket after the final prayer. It occurred to me that all of the perfection that went into the planning of this crushing occasion had absolutely nothing to do with me, other than the music selected. It was handled instinctively by those who had kept their wits about them.

Greeting and thanking hundreds in attendance, some whom I hadn't seen for years, was so supportive and appreciated I was humbled. This was my thing; welcoming and hugging friends. Of course, then I remembered why they were here, tears and embarrassing nose blows stopped me for a moment, only to be followed again by the fake smiles.

Carloads of mourners returned to our home for camaraderie and comfort. Food was spread end to end in the kitchen and dining room. I drifted through the throngs of people astonished that we could get so many of them into our home at one time.

I watched Mike's teammates wolf down the sumptuous meal, and it tore me apart. I remembered, with a shocking pain, the beautiful grin on Mike's face when he saw a spread like this to graze on. He loved food, and I loved feeding him. My God, he must have forgotten how much he loved to eat.

Most of our family stayed on three more days, and it was soothing to have so much love and concern surrounding us. Our minds were kept busy. Our conversations often included happy memories of Mike. Suddenly tears would roll. Just as suddenly, they stopped, and we went on to other subjects.

Neighbors were continually bringing more dishes out of their freezers. Even with Mike's whole team eating dinner, the food just magically kept multiplying, thanks to dedicated friends like Joyce, Donna and Charlie and heaven knows all our friends and neighbors who made things happen.

Friday, September 23, 1994

Our family will all leave today. What am I to do?

Just as suddenly as our family arrived, they flew out that afternoon. We all went out for lunch on the way to the airport, and I think it was the last big occasion I was to enjoy for many years to come. Seeing them board their planes and fly out of our lives jarred me into the stabbing reality of the future ahead of us.

When we got home from the airport and the house was still, grief rolled over me. I envisioned it as a massive steamroller, careening down a steep hill, flattening everything in its path. The screaming emptiness was deadly. Facing a future of never again seeing Mike was just too devastating to comprehend. All I wanted to do was run from it. And we did. We called a friend and asked if we could escape to their lake house for the night. In an hour, we were gone.

OH DEAR MICHAEL.....

You once were and now I'm half not;
I'm trying to thank God; For what I've still got;
We're up in the mountains. I'm blinded with pain;
I'm trying to get through this. It's all so insane;
I miss you so badly. Your void is so vast;
With Christmas behind us, let me lay rest the past;
Let me look at your beauty as though it's still living;
Keep you close in my heart, and find peace in giving;
I will write to remember, and work to forget;
And try to give comfort to others I've met;
Who once were and are now half not

I so love you,
Mom

CHAPTER FIVE

LOOKING BACK

Saturday, September 24, 1994

ONE WEEK TODAY. MIKE IS DEAD! My God. He's just gone. I can't sleep! I can't eat! Help me God, help me.

We awoke early at Nancy and Mike's cottage up at Lake Texoma, having slept on blankets Rod spread on the living room floor. Although there were bunk beds in both bedrooms, Rod wanted to keep holding on to me, because during the week I had slept little and moaned and cried a lot.

On the hour-long drive back home, I frantically planned where I would go for answers to this tragedy. The first place I went was to Mike's room. I poured through each text book and spiral notebook he had, looking for something, anything, which might explain why my boy would have wanted to end his life.

Suddenly. I turned a page in his physiology spiral and found a picture that Mike had drawn. It so shocked me that I thought for a moment, I was going to pass out. It was a picture of a boy who stood with tears rolling down his face, hands raised up helplessly, and a tree, a flower and a cross buried in the green grass. My greatest fear confronted me at this moment. Mike's impulsive decision to end his life wasn't so impulsive after all. He had obviously suffered a profound sadness that he never shared with anyone. And to think Mike and I discussed things all our lives. UNBELIEVABLE.......

There might have been a time, had I only seen this picture sooner, that I could have saved his life. What mother or father wouldn't have recognized the urgency for help, the blatant loss of hope, the untimely doom of the cross? The vivid drawing was the beginning of my *what-ifs and if onlys.* The rest of the day I huddled under my covers, sick with the thought that all the while Mike and I talked about his concerns about schools, baseball, Leslie, much greater fears were over-taking his fragile mind.

Sunday, September 25, 1994

Can't sleep! Can't read! Can't live with this!!

Sandy and I decided to meet at church at 10 a.m. Totally unaware of my speed, I was stopped by a police officer. Here it was, Sunday morning and I was stopped for the first time in my life. He saw my grief and heard my babbling about seeing him at our home when Mike died. That was one of the many crazy things I did for months or maybe years. Why in the world I thought I recognized him in our home is beyond me. But he was kind, patted my arm and told me to be careful. When he drove away, I sat there and sobbed with alarming helplessness.

Monday, September 26, 1994

A letter came for Mike today. Texas A&M accepted him with full senior credit for all of his courses. I fell to my knees. Oh my God. Oh, dear God.

Tuesday, September 27, 1994

A reimbursement check for unused tuition came in the mail today. It was made out to Mike. Seeing his name, as if he were alive, killed me.

The community college efficiently sent back Mike's check since he had withdrawn before the final deadline. Wasn't it just like Mike to want to save us money? It wouldn't surprise me if this was a conscious decision to which he had given considerable thought. Over and over, came the huge waves of shocking pain.

Wednesday, September 28, 1994

Mike sent Mimi a birthday card before he died.

I called my first husband to wish him a good birthday and then called his mom, Mimi to give her love and support. I learned that when she returned home from her week with us there was a birthday card from Mike. He wished her his love, and said he was under a lot of stress trying to get decisions about his future. Of course, we discussed how this could have happened when all of Hillar's family lived through a war in Latvia when Russia invaded and then Germany invaded, and strength ran deep from their harrowing experiences.

Thursday, September 29, 1994

Bought a journal to enter all my horror. Transferring my scribbling from a legal pad of yellow paper, I felt I must keep track of my mind and learn why this happened. It's killing me because I'm not capable of handling reality.

I awoke totally obsessed with finding a book that would explain how a grieving mother survives. I knew I couldn't get through it until I could find answers for this catastrophic event.

I spent four hours looking for a story similar to mine. Nothing at the book stores or library turned up other than medical texts. I tried to explain to one bookstore employee my need for a personal story of recovery after losing your child. I was so fragile I think I scared her to death. At the end of my search there were no words to console me, no clues how to survive day after day.

Friday, September 30, 1994

Rod took me to a recommended psychologist. He sort of led me in, as you would a blind person, to this disgusting, dust-filled, avocado green, waiting room with four colorless, straight-back, vinyl, Mediterranean chairs. I resented the hell out of the man I hadn't yet seen before we entered his personal, dark, cramped, smoke-filled office.

In no time at all, the doctor informed me that my son did this to get back at me. I STOOD RIGHT UP AND WALKED STRAIGHT OUT. My poor surprised husband hastily threw a $100 bill on his nasty, cluttered, 1950's desk. I was just as angry at this ancient total stranger who knew nothing about Mike or me as I was at my husband for paying him one damn cent. I hadn't yet gotten angry at Mike.

Monday, October 3, 1994

I again haunted more bookstores; this time for depression. Was Mike depressed? What did that really mean? Everything was about case studies in medical books. Nothing about a kid who died from an illness you didn't even know he had.

Tuesday, October 11, 1994

Rod and the girls and I attended an SOS meeting (Survivors of Suicide) and we could do nothing but cry. My daughters and I felt totally alienated and simply could not relate. We felt little kinship. We came there to hear about a boy much like Mike; a high achiever, a well-rounded, loving, respectful boy. We were there to learn about another's beloved child taking his life without any outside influences. We wanted help from someone walking in the same shoes. That didn't happen.

Wednesday, October 12, 1994

Who could I call to help me get through this? I learned about two women in the area whose sons had both taken their lives. I called each of them. One, for whom I left a message, never returned my call. The other woman was far too angry over her son's self-inflicted death, because she blamed the police, who put him in jail over night for automobile vandalism. He was so scared, he went home and killed himself over the fear of a future in jail.

She had her own problems to deal with, and the last thing she wanted to do was talk with me. She had been trying to sue the police force for her son's death, and her ongoing rage upset me even more.

I attended Compassionate Friends, a well-known organization for helping people deal with the death of a loved one. I was unable to relate to the depth of another's pain over the loss of an 86-year-old grandmother, a brother-in-law who was sick for years and died from cancer, a husband of seven years who was so addicted to alcohol he died of cirrhosis of the liver.

I went there for a life line that could help me climb out of the dark hole in which I existed. I was there to learn how to find sanity again, despite never having my son back for the rest of my pathetic life. So, I found myself turning inward with my private thoughts. I was a mother in hell living without my *"too good to be true,"* son. The ache of wanting to see, hear, hug the child whom I had nurtured and loved beyond words for twenty-one years was physically debilitating. My every thought screamed, *"Wait a minute...If I could recall the face he made when I suggested that he..." "What did he say the last night we took a long walk, or was it me who did all the talking?" "Why did he insist on doing the dishes the Thursday night after his favorite dinner?" "Wait a minute, wait a minute, I have to think this through again...It's ok...It's ok...It's ok...I can change things if I can only think back to...."*

October 17, 1994

One month ago today, Mike left us for good. I am so slow…I do dumb things. I can't concentrate. My mind is so different than before… Will I ever be able to recover from this shock?

During the first month, I have had horrendous flashbacks of the image of my dead son in the bathtub. They literally jar my head backwards, as if I were being jump-started by an electric shock. Each time the vivid image occurred, I just involuntarily screamed. The shock and jolting pain were simply automatic. But even worse was the ever-present awareness of the total, "*goneness*," of the boy we all loved so much. The fact that we would never again hear his laugh, see his dimpled smile, feel his warm and loving hugs, was so utterly unbelievable, we just couldn't endure the brutal reality.

Besides trying to reconstruct the ending and mentally trying to pinpoint the how's and why's of Mike's death, my solitary mourning consisted mainly of talks with God and Mike. As much as Rod was willing to hear me and hold me, I instead reverted back to bringing Mike back. This unbelievable husband just took charge of absolutely everything. He picked up my share of all of our real estate business and was running himself ragged trying to keep up. We gave all eleven of our files on homes that were scheduled to close to eight of our friends in the office, and they handled all of our business as if it were their own; a really wonderful sacrifice for us.

At some point, I turned to the obituaries each day for consolation. Somehow it calmed me to see a young person who passed away as I knew others were hurting as much as I was. Although I felt badly for the family, I also felt a strange bond with them. Was this another way of looking for someone to relate to? Nothing I did was like the "*old me.*"

I knew that Rod would be incapable of feeling the depth of my pain because he was not Mike's biological father. He had only known him since 1989 when we started dating. He enjoyed when Mike came home from school for holidays and summers. Mike's dad was so distraught, he couldn't even talk about it. I would write him with what I was learning about suicide, but he couldn't go there. So, it was easier to crawl inside myself and go it alone.

During the day to day struggle just to get out of bed and into my comfort chair that Rod had bought me, all senses seemed to have changed. I couldn't feel that anything was familiar anymore. Everything was just so strange to me. I had no desire whatsoever to eat. Concentrating on even the smallest, most mundane issue was impossible. I just preferred to be left alone to think about how to undo all that had been done. So disabled, I felt like an empty shell. I felt like I was honestly losing my mind. I couldn't get enraged about what my son had done. Where had my natural fighting power gone?

Mike and I had never, in his 21 years, ever had an argument. Unreal to think about. Besides, how would I be able to get angry at someone who couldn't have been in his right mind when he did this? Having always been inherently optimistic, my ability to love and forgive my son is what allowed me to continue functioning.

November 1, 1994

Six weeks. Still sending thank you notes to those who brought food and flowers, said mass for Mike, attended our service, planted trees in Mike's memory and who kept vigil over me. I can't watch baseball. It hurts too much. I can't fish. The thought of fishing while my son was dying makes me go limp with instant images of his helplessness.

Friends called to ask how I was getting along. I didn't go to the office anymore because I couldn't deal with telling the story over and over to those who hadn't seen me since Mike died. With 35 agents in our office, the inquiries were endless.

It seems like everyone would say, "I don't know how you're doing it. How can you live with this?" I would respond with a rather cynical, "I wake up in the morning and have two choices; I can either get up, or I can stay in bed. If I get up, eventually, I have to eat. I study books about suicide. Then pretty soon the day is over, and I go to bed and lay there half the night until my shrieking mind rests itself. The next day, it's about the same."

Staying in bed all day wasn't an option. It was too unfair to my husband. If my daughters learned that, it would have killed them to see me disconnecting, detaching myself from reality. Resentment would have built. Bitterness and emptiness would then have won out. I wasn't about to lie down and give up. Besides, I couldn't rest until I had answers. It saved my life.

Saturday, November 5, 1994

It pleased Rod so much when I agreed to go with him to a wedding. There was no way we could know that I would lose it when it suddenly hit me for the first time that Mike would never marry.

With no warning, I began breathing heavily, elephant tears rolled down my cheeks, and I was shaking so hard, I couldn't control myself. Although I fought hard to keep quiet, I felt like the people behind us might have thought I was having a seizure. I felt so physically sick that we had to leave the church and go home.

Sunday, November 6, 1994

I went to a baby shower for a wonderful friend. Christina was having her first child, a baby boy. And she was 42 years of age. I was enjoying meeting her friends and rejoicing for her. With no warning, when she opened her first gift and held up a precious baby blue nightgown with a lamb embroidered on the collar, I completely lost control and ran to the bathroom. When Mike was tiny, I put him in the same nightgown and called him our little lambie. Oh my God, I suddenly remembered, Mike will never be a father. Mike loved babies. Mike forgot he loved babies.

A friend of Christina's who had lost her four-year-old son when he was crossing the street had seen me run for cover. She recognized the horrified reaction on my face, and came into the bathroom to offer a warm hug, and we cried together over the loss of our sons.

Tuesday, November 15, 1994

Leslie called today to say three of Mike's friends had quit college. I was shocked. Their parents didn't want me to know. Mike's death hurt so many people.

Oddly enough, we kept finding coins, mostly dimes. We heard the story about coins in our SOS session. Survivors believe that their deceased loved ones communicate their whereabouts by signaling with the odd placement of a coin. We have found 14-15 coins already.

The glaring coins began when I went into Mike's room to look through all of his books. We had the house cleaned earlier and there were no footprints on the carpet. There, in the middle of his room was a dime. I was stunned. I remembered the movie, *Ghost* and the coin that was moved up the door by Demi Moore's deceased husband, played by Patrick Swayze. As I picked up the coin, I said a prayer to Mike and placed it in a small drawer in Mike's dresser. It may sound weird, but it gave me warmth and hope. What's bad about that?

By now, I had been retreating to *my comfort chair* for over two months. I was still searching for how, why and when everything had gone so wrong. What didn't I see? What hadn't I heard? Where could I have helped more? How could we have all been so blind? Oh, why was I beating myself up so much?

My husband was amazingly patient with me. He hovered, while at the same time, he distanced. He was soft and sympathetic, but supporting and strong. When the great wave washed over me, and I began to breathe heavily, he knew the signal, and took my hand while I squeezed hard until the wave of pain subsided. Every night he would wake me from my hideous nightmares and hold me so closely. He put up with my subconscious moans, and spooned with me as I cried myself back to sleep.

Shortly before Thanksgiving, I began to realize the futility of trying to reconstruct the past. I was finally learning that there was no point in trying to determine whether I had listened closely enough, offered too much advice, didn't ask enough of the right questions or didn't wait for the full answers.

Instead of trying to bring Mike back to earth by solving an unsolvable hidden answer, I made a determined effort to realize that whatever forced Mike to the brink may never be made evident to us, and that he wanted it that way, or had no power over his deteriorating mind.

Around the third week of November, the giant waves of pain came often. Mike won't be home for Thanksgiving. Picking him up from the airport when he came home from college was one of the biggest joys of my life.

November 24, 1994

Thanksgiving Day. Crushing time for us. No airport, no Mike. Rod and I met Sue and Matt and Sandy and Jim at the cemetery. Leaves were falling silently on his burial site. Mike's granite marker had just been laid, and was a shock to see our son's name, birth and death date and the symbolic crossed baseball bats and ball; the telltale sign of the love of his life.

Sandy held Thanksgiving dinner at her apartment to divert our attention from the norm. It was a valiant effort, but we were all faking it to keep it light. I had written a prayer to read at dinner, but couldn't get through it without sobbing, and later, wished I hadn't felt the need to compose and read it. Sue really broke down, but in retrospect, since she kept so much inside, I was glad she finally broke down and let it out.

After dessert, we split up the uneaten food (and there was a lot of it with Mike not eating), and went home with hugs and a sense that nothing would ever be the same again.

I couldn't help but wonder if a mother can love too much. I never read that, but now I doubted everything I did or didn't do. Where were my instincts? Where was God before the unthinkable happened? Did He not see the trouble ahead and want to warn me? WHY?...

I began to notice I was very depressed about Christmas. I felt sick every day. How could we possibly celebrate Christmas without Mike? Just when I thought I was improving, I was back in denial. I asked the most unbelievable question of Rod. "Oh my God, what is Mike eating? Who is feeding him?"

"Oh Annie, they don't eat like we do...." I knew that. Why in the world had I thought that? Was I completely losing my mind? I realized then how extremely fragile and helpless I was. I just didn't have any will to live, and I felt if I died, it just might be easier anyway.

December 13, 1994

Sleepless nights. I pray Mike sends me a signal that he is ok. I've put Christmas off as long as I can. I must make myself look for presents for our other kids. We must get a tree. I must try harder......

I discussed depression with a client who had attempted to take her life jumping off her apartment balcony. She was a nurse and didn't even recognize her own symptoms. She said if Mike was so full of anguish with all of his decisions about Leslie, colleges, medical specialty fields, he may have killed himself out of sheer panic and anxiety.

Leslie's mom shared with us that she thought of taking her life several times, and felt that perhaps she and Mike both suffered from a chemical imbalance. This was the only sensible answer we heard to explain why an intelligent, loving, caring boy would devastate his family and friends so cruelly, when during his whole life he displayed so much love and respect for all of us.

December 18, 1994

Rod got me to my feet and we went to a department store and bought item after item for each of our five children and their significant others. Christmas was now going to happen.

Rod felt we should go to a Christmas tree farm to pick out our tree. We wandered around aimlessly searching for just the right tree and finally settled on a big, bushy, white pine.

When we got home and Rod unraveled the tree from its netting, we were amazed at its size. Its outstretched branches literally filled more than half of our small family room. Any other time we would have laughed heartily at our mistake in judgment. This time I totally freaked out. I screamed and sobbed and ranted and raved and hated my husband and Christmas and God and myself. This was not a pretty sight.

Rod solemnly turned around, marched the huge tree out and brought it through the front door, placed it in front of the living room window, and that was the only Christmas we had two trees.

The gigantic pine ended up taking every strand of lights we owned, as well as each and every ornament we had between us. It forced me out of the house to pursue a smaller tree for the family room. I got a slender, little six-foot scotch pine and decorated it with white lights and 50 beige, knit angels. Throughout its branches, I floated yards of glorious ivory, open weave, waffled ribbon that gave the tree a spiritual effect.

I poured us a glass of wine, sat down, lit a dear angel candle Rod had given me one afternoon, and for the next two weeks, I lived for this time in front of the angel-inspired tree each night. I found peace and some happiness. Rod whispered tenderly, "That's one in a row."

December 25, 1994

Mike was the best part of Christmas for 21 years. He was our baby. The girls loved being with him. Hillar is here. He's filled with rage. I am just sick. I can't get angry. He can't stop. OH, DEAR GOD......

We snacked, opened gifts, talked and made a warm environment for our daughters. We held on to one another in a circle, and sent up Mylar balloons as we silently said a prayer in tribute to Mike. It brought a sense of calm and purpose as we watched the balloons twinkle in the sun for what seemed like miles.

When the balloons disappeared, we all hugged and felt better than we had in weeks. Bret and Jill came, and after dinner, Mike's closest friends, Bill, Steve, Jamie and Julie all came. The surprise was so overwhelmingly appreciated. Some of our close friends also joined us that night. Tears, smiles and stories of cherished memories got us through Christmas minus Mike.

December 26, 1994

Our second anniversary. Quiet and thoughtful. Have to keep moving. Need to have something in which to look forward.

December 31, 1994

New Year's Eve with friends at a quiet dinner party. Toasted to a year ahead of just trying to keep on keeping on.

January 1, 1995

Football, football, football—and no Mike. This is just unreal. This has been Mike's favorite day since he was ten years old, and he and his dad and I watched games from morning to night.

Leslie flew in from Mobile to spend the weekend. Sue and Sandy came and we all spent the day talking and sleeping a lot. We seemed to say, "Hmmmm," after anything was said about Mike. We could not come to any conclusions about anything, so we just continued to say, "Hmmmmm" to show we were still involved in the conversation, but too mush-minded to say anything intelligent or thought provoking.

January 15, 1995

Every time I turn on the TV, depression seems to be the subject. Was it like when you were pregnant, all you saw were pregnant women? Or when you had stopped smoking, every person you saw in a car had a cigarette in his hand. Depression, anxiety and suicide weren't discussed much before 1998. The importance of checking symptoms of mental illness wasn't on TV like drug information was. I never knew a thing about depression. I thought it was like crying all day, not getting out of bed, never smiling or having fun.

Why hadn't Mike just said, "Something is wrong with me, Mom. I think I need help." Who am I kidding? He did say many, many times that summer that he couldn't make decisions.

He couldn't concentrate. He couldn't sleep. My only problem was that I didn't have the ability to know what those problems meant. That inability cost me my son's life.

Drugs was the biggest concern during the eighties, nineties and ever since. But our son didn't travel in that world. All of our assumptions that Mike would *"get over it,"* were so wrong. Dead Wrong.

By the end of January, I made a vow to become stronger, and try to put Mike's death behind me in the year to come. Each day the first two weeks of January I kept telling my mind that it was going to be better tomorrow, much like trying to go on a diet tomorrow, and you mean it, but it just doesn't happen for you.

I thought there could be no greater grief than with the loss of my parents. But with their death, I felt abandoned. When Mike died, I didn't just feel dead, as far as I could tell, the me I had always known was truly dead. I had lost 95% of my capacity for emotional response, other than the never-ending sense of doom. Life no longer seemed to have color. I was in a trance like state. I didn't hear music. I didn't feel joy. I only felt heavy breathtaking pain and a constant sense of dread.

I was numb day after day, just gazing into space. But oh, what a trip my busy, frantic mind was on, still trying so hard to figure it all out. I wouldn't have spent so many hours working on the solution if my unsound, shell-shocked mind hadn't honestly believed I could bring Mike back somehow. Just unimaginable how messed up my mind seemed to be. When will I ever have joy back into my life? How am I going to cope the rest of my days? I can't do this. I don't see any way I can ever get through this. I NEED HELP, GOD. I NEED HELP!

February 2, 1995

My day begins and ends with thoughts of Mike. There is virtually no escape from the instant mind flashes of my son dead in the bathtub. Now when I start to get frantic, I silently say, "It's ok, it's ok, it's ok. Just like calming a scared child or puppy.

I found I had turned into a recluse. I did take clients out occasionally to look at homes, but most of the time, I represented sellers in marketing their homes because I could work more efficiently in the privacy and peace and quiet of our home office. It saved me a lot of painful conversations, but at the same time, many friends in my office missed seeing me and hearing my familiar happy laugh. I missed that laugh more than anyone could know.

By accident one day, I discovered the value of being alone in the car. While coming home from showing property one foggy, dreary night, the instant flashback of discovering Mike dead in the tub hit with its usual unexpected vengeance. I opened my mouth and just screamed and screamed. I needed that. I found I had become so cautious in keeping my killing pain to myself so as not to alarm Rod, the solitary screaming turned out to be the best release of anguish I had found yet.

The medical examiner called me back to answer the questions that had just recently surfaced on my mind. Had it really taken almost five months before I had any medical questions about Mike? By then I had read several books about chemical imbalance in the brain, and that was the nature of my questions.

According to the medical examiner, Mike's bloodwork had been negative for harmful substances. He felt that perhaps his nerve endings had no receptors, but there was no method of testing the chemistry in his brain after death. I read somewhere that it is common and quite essential to search for some meaning and justification to help rid the pain and begin recovering.

When you begin to find meaning, you question everything. You seek even the smallest detail. You are trying to make sense of it all, but something that makes no sense isn't always answered.

You often learn as much as possible about the afterlife. It actually allowed me to picture something besides the gruesome ending of my son's life. It helped bridge the unfamiliar, painful disconnection. It helped bring a positive picture to my mind and that was exactly what I was hungering for.

I realized that I now had no fear whatsoever about my own death. I almost looked forward to it, for it was the only sure way I could ever again be joined with my deceased child. Later, I learned that was not the only way.

February 11, 1995

Today, a young girl is coming here to tell me about her final thoughts before she swallowed a bottle of pills. Maybe I can get some understanding to ease my so sick mind

I was very grateful for her honesty and time. She swallowed an entire bottle of aspirin around the hour of 3 a.m. Her mother usually woke her at 7 a.m. for school, but this next particular morning her mom awoke at 6 a.m. and for some inexplicable reason, went to check on her daughter. When she couldn't wake her from her deep sleep, she called 911, and God chose to leave her on earth to learn more lessons.

When Lisa began her story, I was stunned, never having heard a story of the mental breakdown of a successful, seemingly happy young person. She was on the dean's list, the vice-president of her high school class and a popular member of the drill team. She felt well liked and had a bubbly personality. But underneath she was disappointed in herself and unhappy.

Lisa said she put extreme pressure on herself and didn't know why. She didn't want to worry her mom because she had seen how many worries her mom had always dealt with in the course of her broken marriage and raising three kids alone.

Being a people-pleaser, she was terrified that she would disappoint her parents, teachers and coach if she let them know how she really felt about herself. She never thought about trying to please herself. She had a lot of guilt that she wasn't going to be what others expected. To add to her internal grief, she was angry at herself because she couldn't get a handle on things.

The seventeen-year old carried the idea of killing herself for about a year. She knew her parents would be sad, but that they would eventually get over it and be better off without all of her privately held problems. She gave absolutely no thought to the future and didn't think for a minute about what she would be missing. She had no feel, no direction and was consumed only with a negative attitude and what a disappointment she was to herself.

Because her mind would not stop racing with the problems she couldn't solve, she couldn't sleep more than a few hours at a time. That night her total exhaustion brought her to the final decision. At 3 a.m. Lisa reached for the bottle that would take all of her anguish away.

I sat there breathless. It sounded like a record I had played; a movie I had seen. Michael could have been sitting here telling the exact story. It was easy to imagine that the last thing he wanted to do was worry me anymore with all of his indecision and fears. I felt that he would have been disgusted with himself for not getting a handle on all the things that bothered him so much that summer.

I got the message loud and clear. The whole picture came into focus. Something took over Mike's brain that allowed him to take his life and end the pain. Being a perfectionist, he did the job all too well.

How exhausting it must have been for our son while trying to decide whether to choose life or death. What an overwhelming decision it must have been to take total control of his pain.

What was his last thought on earth? Did he pray? Did peace find its way at the last moment? How truly kind of Mike not to have placed the gun to his head. How much more shocking and horrifying that would have been for me.

February 17, 1995

How will I ever feel joy again? I counted my blessings that we always let one another know we loved them daily. I remembered how others suffered the guilt when they lost a loved one and hadn't really gotten around to telling them how much they cared about them.

I suspect that Mike suffered guilt for not living up to his own expectations of himself. All through school and sports we tried to teach him he didn't have to be the best; just do the best he could and enjoy it. Did he ever believe that failure was expected as well? Or were his expectations so high and his disappointments so vast that the charade began when he was young?

February 20,1995

We learned today that our son, Mikel and Melissa are having a baby. I lost it. It hit me that Mike would never have children. Instead of being thrilled for them, I was crushed. What was the matter with me? Seeing moms with their sons upset me. I was going through McDonalds drive-through when I looked at my rearview mirror and saw a mom and her son, maybe about 12, laughing together in their car. I kept looking at them as tears rolled down my cheeks. Mike and I had such fun times together after I picked him up from school and took him shopping or somewhere to feed his hungry face.

March 17, 1995

I am alarmed at my mental helplessness. I must get stronger. It encouraged me to say to myself, "Mike knew how much we loved him. He always knew he could tell us anything. His brain must have kept a secret from him and from us.

His brain was chemically ill. God will keep him safe and peaceful now." It helped. It really helped.

I began to believe that Mike was simply not dead. Dead was dead. And I realized once I got away from that thought, I might survive. I knew he had transitioned to a higher place, but he was so in my heart and head, so much a part of my life, I felt and knew that he was truly alive in spirit and that one realization helped me to get better, keep sane and keep going forward.

March 30. 1995

The thing I notice most about myself is that I have no sparkle.

Once I had such zest for life. I wonder if that will ever return? My health is so compromised. I keep getting infections. I seem to be falling apart. But my spirit, Mike, is right there helping me keep my faith in God and my future. This is my salvation.

April, 1995

We're in San Francisco visiting our best friends, Pam and Gabe.

I have to get happy again. Mike would only want that for all of us. I must try harder and keep remembering how lucky I am to have Sue and Sandy. What would I have done if I had only one child?

Mother's Day, 1995

Oh God, I no longer am the mother of a living son. I miss Mike. I kind of ride on a wave that takes me here and there with no feeling one way or the other. When Mike said he had no feeling, I wish I had known it was depression. I must have depression! Did I honestly just discover this? All I do is sob. I'm cold and uncaring. I am so damn numb. How can Rod even stand me?

We all went to breakfast and then to the cemetery to put fresh flowers on Mike's grave. A lot of tears were shed together. I wish I could make this easier for our daughters.

Memorial Day, 1995

A day to honor our deceased-a day so many others have mourned since day one. Please God, help me to see what I can do to help others. What can I do to educate someone to not let this happen to other kids? How can I make Mike's life have meaning? I've got to do something besides die thinking of Mike being so totally gone from us.

June, 1995

Oh Mike, did you die because you lost your hope and dreams? Did you fear the future? Did you feel you were a failure? Did you really not have faith in God? Did you suffer from a chemical imbalance? Or was all of this really over Leslie returning home? Son, how is it that you didn't love life? I taught you to love God and yourself first, then you would know how to love others. Did you never believe me? Were you like your dad, believing the scientific aspects of our world's origin? How very different your dad and I saw things. Was your dad a true atheist, or had all of the fears he developed, growing up in a war-torn environment, convinced him there really couldn't have been a God? Were you secretly believing like dad after living with him your last few years?

June 22, 1995

We've sold this house where we lost our son. We're building a new home in Plano and the address adds up to 7. Mike's number in life from the month he was born, to the day he was born, to his baseball numbers and so much more. God is master-minding our plan. I am letting Him take care of me slowly, but I know, surely.

July 7, 1995

Twenty-two years ago today, our dearest only baby boy was born. The cord was wrapped around his little neck and he did not receive all of my antibodies. Did something important die in his brain when oxygen was cut off by the cord constriction? Perhaps in some way, his birth was responsible for his death. We will never know. When the firsts of everything go by, I feel I will be stronger and more able to go forward. Won't I?

August 9, 1995

Today I spent hours in Mike's room packing things away. I am finally attending to all of Mike's belongings, bits and pieces, remembrances, happy memories and scary reminders. There are a few pieces of clothing that I can bury my nose in, and feel that the scent of my son is still alive. Tomorrow we move out. Bittersweet but hopeful.

August 10, 1995

This last morning I walked from room to room seeing Mike. With coffee in hand, I thought about our last days together. I saw you in the recliner, lying on the leather couch, studying (or so I thought) on your bed, diving into our pool after mowing lawns all day, and dying in the tub of our bathroom. I'm moving away from this house of great loss.

September 17, 1995

Mike left us forever a year ago today. The firsts are over. I'm telling myself I'm going over the mountain. I must concentrate only on happy memories. No going back. Only up and forward.

October, 1995

Oddly enough, Hillar is also building a new home in Orlando. I feel as if we are both trying to rebuild our lives. I am throwing myself into each and every inch of this build-job with all the energy and love I can muster. Mike is by my side every step of the way.

Christmas, 1995

A blur. No feelings of warmth or excitement. We all tried. Christmas was about Sandy coming home from college. Then Mike coming home from college. Now it's about getting through the day as quickly as possible. Sliding backwards.... Thinking too much about Mike's entirely screwed up interpretation of himself. How could it happen when we raised him with so much love and communication and honesty? Stop it! Stop it!

January, 1996

My poor devastated daughters. They grieve differently.
One can't talk about it. The other calls me and we try so hard to figure out when it all went so badly so fast.

February 1996

Jill and Rodney were married, and our family was happy. We danced and laughed and it honestly felt wonderful to be normal for a night.

March, 1996

We moved into our beautifully built, lovingly planned home. Complete with the plaque of angels we had built into the brick. Michael, you have been with us every single day.

April 1996

Our first grandson, Colin was born.

Once again, our family was thrilled for our children. A glimmer of hope continues.

May, 1996

Sandy and Jim were married and our families rejoiced together.

We feel stronger, and feel like Mike is working with God like a well-oiled wheel, taking us closer and closer towards a life of peace and happiness.

July 7, 1996

Mike's birthday is today. He would be twenty-three today. His birthday is always hard to get past, but not as difficult as the day of his death.

September 17, 1996

Mike has been gone from us for two years. Reading constantly, I'm learning a lot about depression and anxiety and taking notes.

November, 1996

What is the matter with me? I'm crying every day. Mike is my first thought in the morning and the last thought in the night; automatic. Can't help it.

January, 1997

Bret and Carolyn's beautiful baby, Savannah, arrived.

Christmas, 1997

It is so good to have children around at Christmas. We did really well this year. Is it coming around full circle?

May, 1998

By divine guidance from God, we bought a home in Granbury, TX.

We took a day's pleasure trip to a town I had once shown property in the 1980s. It was Mother's Day and I didn't want to talk on the phone to anyone in real estate. We happened to turn at the right gated community, saw the lake, drove by a house with a small sign out front, called to see it, and our lives changed in less than an hour when we gave the owner a $3,000 deposit to hold it until we could go to a local real estate office and type up a contract.

July, 1998

Mike would be 25 today. I feel him all around us. As we fish on the dock, fly on the boat, water ski, have drinks on the deck, we are truly having a good time and I am not missing Mike nearly as much here in this very different setting.

August, 1998

Baby Ryan Davis joined Mike in heaven. Tough time for all.

Our third little grandbaby, Ryan arrived several weeks early to the dismay of his parents, Mikel and Melissa, Colin and Pappy and me. He was stillborn. And a few days later, we laid him to rest in the tiniest white casket and once again felt that heavy sense of painful sorrow.

September, 1998

Mike left us four years ago. Still keeping my journal. Writing my thoughts over the years even inspires me to think about maybe writing. Something like that might give my life a new direction—on Mike's behalf.

Christmas, 1998

Here at the lake. Much easier pace. Doing so much better. We are doing really well, and true joy is creeping in.

February, 1999

Our third little grandbaby, Hunter, was born in January.

We just returned from San Diego, bonding with the little guy. He watches everything Savannah does with such contentment. Once again, babies are the healing joy coming back.

May 9, 1999

My personal, first grandson, Sean Michael came into this world today. It's such a thrill for Sandy and Sue, Hillar and me to have our very own little baby at last. He is mending my heart as if he were sent by God for this purpose. This miracle baby was developed by invitro fertilization when that method of procreation wasn't that well known or perhaps that successful.

September 15, 1999

I'm at the lake to get past Mike's day of death. I have gone through my whole journal, and am surprised at how I have actually improved in five years. I'm seriously contemplating putting all of our experiences and thoughts into a book. Never having found a book about a drug-free, alcohol-fee, high-achiever taking his own life, I had to spend years looking for answers.

Maybe if I could write a book about all that I have learned involuntarily, as an uninformed victim, I could personally show parents and kids how to detect depression and anxiety before the horrifying act of suicide occurs. No family should have to go through the hell of losing a child, particularly when the loss is a result of unknown mental pain resulting in suicide.

September 16, 1999

Rod just called and told me to pack and come home.

He made reservations to fly to San Francisco tomorrow, when it will be five years to the day when Mike left us. What a wonderful man I married seven years ago. How thoughtful could he be?

September 17, 1999

We are in San Francisco and having such a great day.

What a wonderful surprise that even my daughters knew about it and kept it secret. In just 12 hours, we've already witnessed a SWAT team run through our hotel lobby to get to the roof of our building. Armed with high-powered rifles, they were there to protect U.S. Vice President Al Gore, who was speaking at a luncheon across the street. Then, in a restaurant overlooking the bay, a parade of yachts honored the woman president of Ireland, seated at the table next to us. WILD!

September 17, 1999

(More) hours later, we had cocktails in our hotel lobby. Relaxing after a day of shopping, were Vicky Lawrence of the Carol Burnett Show and her husband. I wrote a one-liner expressing love for her role and her sense of humor.

My husband absolutely refused to pass it over. I'm sure he saved them from yet another intrusive fan. On the other hand, I had visions of joining them at their table for some good conversation. Was this just me?

Although Mike has been gone five years today, it's been the very best of the very worst of days, and I'm feeling really good about my progress. I have prayed for strength and guidance from God for so long, and all along the way, I've known He and Mike were there with me.

October, 1999

Our second little granddaughter, Allison, was born a preemie.

And a mighty little, red-haired girl was she. Mikel and Melissa have been blessed after losing Ryan the year before. Five little grandbabies bring lots of smiles and joy into our lives.

December, 1999

Rod had emergency surgery for an impacted colon.

This was a quiet Thanksgiving and Christmas as Rod has been ill since the end of October. How lucky we are that he did not have cancer, which, unknown to us, was suspected by this surgeon.

April, 2000

Sandy and Jim surprised us tonight that they are expecting again.

We were thrilled to hear tonight at a fun family dinner, that Sean will be having a brother or sister, next November. Wow! Six grandbabies in less than four years. Thank you, GOD.

September 17, 2000

We stayed home and handled the date of Mike's death.

We handled it? We? I handled it. It's six years now. My day wasn't ruined. I am conquering the battle for real.

October, 2000

The doctors have moved Sandy and Jim's due date up. Worries me.

They discovered the placenta is blocking the baby from being able to come through the birth canal. She is scheduled to have a C-section October 25, and we are to be blessed with our fourth grandson.

October 25, 2000

Our little Blake Nolan arrived picture-perfect

All I could do was to cry from the relief of stress and worry with our daughter's complications and with overwhelming gratefulness to God for yet another blessed, new, healthy baby in our life.

December, 2000

We had a wonderful Christmas. Everyone is healthy.

All the children are growing beautifully. I babysit every moment I can, in addition to trying to keep up with my journal and selling real estate. Here's to 2001. I must do something with all that I have learned. I must make everyone aware of the hidden aspects of suicide.

December, 2001

Shockingly, my query letter was read and my manuscript pursued by a literary agency in Del Mar, CA. Ultimately, it was rejected, but the president of the company wrote a personal letter with a great deal of advice and suggestions to continue pursuing other companies.

Late in January, 2003

My mammogram suggested a sonogram for a better look. Instincts told me it didn't look good for me. A biopsy was taken and we waited from a Thursday to the next Tuesday for the results. My left breast had malignant cells, which required surgery.

I sprang into action immediately, calling two of my friends for advice about their doctors. I made appointments with both of their doctors and within a week we were well into the procedures required to look at my overall health, lymph node involvement, tumor location, and more.

My oncologist asked if I had experienced trauma eight or so years prior to his analysis of my cancer cells. It indicated approximately that length of time when free radicals attacked my immune system. The question shocked me. How did he know? I burst into tears and told him that Michael took himself out of this world. He hugged and hugged me and let me weep until I needed tissue. Then it was business. Important business.

As a result of the malignancy, I had two lumpectomies on my left breast, each resulting in additional malignant cells outside the margins taken in surgery. Pretty much petrified us. My husband and I agreed with my doctor that a double mastectomy/bi-lateral would end any fear of another malignancy in my right breast in the future.

My third surgery involved the mastectomy and preparation for breast implants; the perk I felt I deserved to bring back the pretty abundant breasts I had lost. The fourth surgery occurred after many months of infections and recovery and was done to remove the medical equipment placed in my chest to create space for the addition of the implants.

We decided it was time for me to smell the roses, retire from real estate, sell our home and move from our location in Plano, Texas, to our Lake Granbury waterfront home. The house sold in one day, and in May, 2003, we took everything possible to Lake Granbury and leased an apartment in West Plano to finish the year and close out our business.

The fifth surgery was the inclusion of my implants in September, 2003. In little more than two days, I was in tremendous pain with a terribly swollen chest, breast implants protruding almost to my neck and fierce infection fluids projecting from my breasts. We raced madly to the hospital in Dallas from Granbury at 4 a.m. and an emergency sixth surgery was performed to remove the totally rejected foreign bodies introduced into my savaged body.

Almost immediately, I was completely out of pain and ready to heal from almost a year of physical and mental pain. By the way, the two friends I called for recommendations both died of cancer that year. As it turned out, I was such a blessed woman in spite of all the pain and disappointment. At least I was healthy and alive.

July 20, 2005

Our beautiful red haired, Cameron Mikel Rowan was born.

What a thrill to once again be the grandparents of a baby. Could never get enough of all of our babies. Jill and Rodney are beside themselves with happiness since the little fellow took 10 years to get here.

February, 2009

My health was great. Suddenly Rod's wasn't.

I retired from real estate in January 2004 and began an interesting career of writing a weekly column for our gated community, which had become an incorporated city of its own. I wrote the De Cordova Bend Estates news column for the Hood County News from 2004 to 2008, hustling from meeting to meeting to be able to report how our city was progressing.

Then came the news from Rod's doctor that Rod had prostate cancer. Several visits to doctors, opinions from his male friends, personal discussions and decisions, he chose the method of controlling the disease most comfortable to him mentally and physically.

He was operated on by a physician from Germany whom we felt was a genius and who introduced his up-and-coming robotic non-intrusive operating system to remove his prostate. He was a savior to us. Regardless of the high demand for his services, he gave us his personal cell phone number for questions. Everything went perfect and our life returned to calmness.

September, 2011

I revisited my manuscript and began to rewrite. So many more suicides were being publicized, I was obsessed with rewriting my information for the third time.

I had taken up oil painting completely out of a coincidence in 2006 and loved it so much. I concentrated mainly on the relaxation from my new hobby. In a chance moment in time, I was trying on a dress that had a lining. In the dressing room, I found myself with my arms up, totally stuck in between the lining and the dress. All I could do was to laugh hysterically.

The sweet, elderly owner of the boutique heard me and offered to help me when I told her of my circumstances. We laughed so hard, she said, "You would be so fun to paint with!" All I could picture, and it was difficult, was that she must paint houses with Habitat for Humanity.

She laughed when I asked if that was what she meant, and said, "No silly, I have a room in the back and teach students how to paint." I laughed right back and said, "I would be your worst nightmare in a painting class, I can't do more than draw a stick figure."

With the immediate purchase of materials from her little boutique artist's shelving, I picked a lovely, peaceful picture to paint. It included a chapel, waterfall, wooden fence, lots of trees, and a ruddy, weed-lined road, stopping at the stairway to a church. I added a cross in the ground giving spiritual recognition and remembrance of the son we lost.

With little help from my darling 90-year-old artist mentor, I painted a Thomas Kinkade look-alike shocking us both with my unknown ability. Since I also played the piano by "ear," it seemed as if

God graced me with many wonderful gifts.

June, 2016

A publishing company wants my manuscript! And now, the greatest coincidence, which really isn't a coincidence at all, occurred when I attended a weekly Tuesday night writers seminar. It was offered by the minister of Thistle Ridge Church, C.C. Risenhoover, who was also a published author of many widely read books. The third Tuesday, he invited a publisher to give some advice to the 18 or so students in our class.

After the question-and-answer series was completed, the publisher happened to be standing by my chair and noticed I had a rather thick, clip-bound manuscript with me. He asked, "Is this something you have written?" I replied, "Yes." He asked, "What is this about?" and I answered, "About losing my son to suicide." That was another "God-thing."

He read the manuscript on his return trip to Oklahoma and called me the next day saying, "I want to publish it."

And now, here we are. Please let my cluelessness in 1994, cry for your AWARENESS and process it deeply in your mind. Save your kids, save yourself from unseen, unheard depression, and anxiety. LOOK, LISTEN AND ASK QUESTIONS requiring more than a simple yes or no answer. Ask your child's friend if he's acting different. SEEK MEDICAL ADVICE, COMMUNICATE YOUR LOVE AND CONCERN, and don't be at all afraid that DISCUSSING SUICIDE will put the idea in your child's head. IT'S BEEN THERE, TRUST ME. AND TO BELIEVE OTHERWISE IS DEAD WRONG

(2017)

Lost a year with a fraudulent publisher who is under indictment

Seasons of Grief

In the fall, I miss you most of all;
Like the leaves fly away, you flew away...
And the winter, bleak and gray, brings an even harder day;
For warmth of fire and Christmas cheer are simply gone for me this
year...
The growth of spring is the toughest thing;
For you are no longer growing; You are gone inevitably forever...
The summer comes with joy to some; but not to me, for I am numb;
I miss your smile, your loving ways; I look for you in all my days...
And oh, those nights; how hard they are;
For you have truly gone afar;
I know God holds you in his hand; I'll see you in another land...

December, 1995
I love you, Mike
—Mom

CHAPTER SIX

~~~

GRIEF

GRIEF IS THE natural process a person who has lost a love, a way of life or another debilitating event from which they are trying to recover. No two people grieve the same way and there is no limit of time from which to emerge from each of its stages. Women openly pour out their grief most often, while men, on the other hand clam up, keeping their grief to themselves. Pain accompanies grief and it presents itself in stages; shock, denial, anger, bargaining, depression and acceptance.

Mothers who lose a child may recall and disassemble every single response, body language or facial reaction during the final days or weeks of their child's life. They try to analyze the devastation by pinpointing when, where, how and why their child is forever gone. This was the path I took. I was so disoriented I thought in short bits. So, I would start over to find a way to bring my son back from death.

Fathers, during a crisis, shut down and block out everything in order to survive. This was Mike's dad. They often fight back not only to survive, but never show any weakness. Dads tend to become bitter and very angry and return to work to separate the pain and forget the event entirely

Analyzing the minute details of the death of our child is perhaps the process that helps us survive. Facing the issues that sent us into chaos is what keeps our brain working. And reliving the horror to determine the answers actually sent me toward acceptance because I eventually had to surrender to the unknown details and understand that I would truly never know for sure the why in the equation.

The automatic first stage of grief after the death of our child is shock and denial; total disbelief, confusion, helplessness, alarm and great fear. Shock is a tremendous trauma that is not acknowledgeable in order to protect us from the reality of the fact. Sometimes we deny the reality of the death by actually attempting to resurrect the child by changing an event, a remark, a feeling, a mistake or a moment in time which resulted in our child's death. I tried to bring Mike back by pinpointing an incident where I could have saved him from his catastrophic decision. And I worked on changing the outcome for weeks.

When in shock, we are virtually often frozen in place with little ability to function. We think and act in slow motion and can't react or respond. We fear losing our other children, being alone and abandonment. I experienced each of these fears. So did my daughters. Our memory may fail, our speech follows heavy sighs, and we seem to be on the outside looking in. Shock and denial help us to survive through numbness because nothing makes sense around us. They end up helping us to cope in stages and is actually nature's way of controlling what we can take in and handle. Eventually, the shock and denial fade away and you begin to realize you are slowly healing through the grief process.

When the numbness fades, you are suddenly aware that all of the chaotic moments and excruciating pain are for real. Your whole life has changed forever, and you have no idea of how to go on.

This awareness brings on guilt, constant stress, loss of personal control of emotions and a sense of doom and fear. You think nothing matters anymore; you don't care if you eat, sleep or even go on living. You lose your strength, your sense of security and your mental ability as well as your physical ability to carry on. Anger, depression and anxiety seem to overtake your days and nights.

Anger is a common and necessary stage in the grief process. When the reality begins to sink in, whether silently or outwardly you feel deeply hurt, mad, enraged at the outcome, the child or young adult who died, yourself, friends of your dead child, your family and even God. It is a manageable emotion and strengthens you as you heal. The pain in anger is horrendous because it reminds you of the overwhelming loss and frightening future. The anger you feel is always an indication of the depth of your love.

You may find that you are jealous of other couples who have not lost a child, or you're silently hurt and angry at friends who didn't attend the funeral, didn't pitch in to help with food, prayers, plans, or even just calling to tell you they are there for you when you break down. This stage usually doesn't last a long time, but dissipates as you try to accept the reality and find ways to get through each moment, day, week and month.

The pain of awareness is often so tortuous and exhausting and often promotes a weakened immune system, which contributes to excess sickness. You just want to withdraw from life. You begin to hibernate because you are so full of never ending despair and performing anything above and beyond the basic functions is not worth the effort simply because nothing matters much.

Withdrawal is easy so you can run away from the reality. Many lose their self-esteem and feel so helpless that they fantasize away the hurt through constant memories of happy memories. Survivors often lose a lot of weight, but others gain weight. Many stop taking care of themselves and suffer physical disorders such as back problems, headaches, vomiting, constipation and insomnia. When exercise stops, eating is almost impossible and sleep falls to a minimum, suicide survivors are treading dangerously. Experiencing joy is almost impossible and the future looks bleak. Mood swings become prevalent as we try to climb out of the bottomless pit and over a monumental mountain to eventual acceptance

Acceptance comes as we run out of alternatives. We begin to take control of ourselves, and try to become conscious of forgiving and trying to forget for periods of a time. We try to bring closure to the pain and start taking a path to a new positive direction with a different identity from that we had before life as we knew it changed 360 degrees. Outside circumstances begin to bring back some happiness, self-esteem, confidence and perhaps joy.

A new baby in the family, another of your children marry, you receive a promotion, you find a more fulfilling job, you meet a mate if you are divorced, and several other circumstances take ahold of you and present a saving influence. Along the way, one or many events aid in healing you. This could happen within a year or two, or take a lifetime to truly heal. No matter the time limit, healing is in your future at some point with some slow progress or repeated changes in good fortune. Seven babies, buying a home on a beautiful lakeside, several weddings of our daughters, a loving and strong partnership with my husband and God all combined together to bring me back to a life full of joy.

Accept that you will never be the same after the death of your child, and life will require that you find meaning, direction and purpose in moving forward so that your child's death was not in vain. Do something for others, put yourself among children your child's age, volunteer with children's organizations, offer a scholarship in your child's name, join survivor groups to contribute spreading awareness of the depression that precedes suicide.

You can now accept your loss. You accept your pain. You accept your new self and your new place in life. You can look forward to replacing hurt with hope. And now, life can truly begin again.

Our renewal brings a stronger us. Time and faith brought us

through the long, difficult and crushing struggle. Hope is restored and a new passion may well begin. The period of healing existed about six years for me. I know this because of the journal I kept. I know this because of the years of reading about anxiety, depression, suicide and renewed belief that I could go forward. The passion I acquired was to alert all to watch for hidden depression, listen to answers when you learn how to ask the right questions of your kids. Get medical help quickly if crisis exists for you and/or your child.

Grief support through counseling individually or among community support groups is available to all when you feel you need help in recovering. But the support on a daily basis demands empathy and compassion of your family as well as your friends.

So many people feel so inadequate because they just don't know what to say to the aggrieved survivor. These friends or acquaintances simply need to know that not a single word is even necessary. Just offering their hand, a hug, a sympathy card, flowers, prayers through the church and even a voice mail or internet message is always so much better than nothing.

Expressing your thoughts, feelings, concerns or love at least lets the suffering person know that she or he is not alone, and that others care enough to take the time to show their emotions. Even if one is too afraid to bring up the subject, or scared they will say all the wrong things, any attempt to offer comfort far surpasses totally ignoring the survivor. Any mention at all is of great comfort to the grieving person. And in the process of healing, talking about your lost loved one is essential to keeping hope and love alive.

Writing in my journal was my greatest source of pouring out my grief, without intruding into another's time and space. Friends planted a tree for our son and it was healing to watch it grow year after year. I saw a lovely shadow box which held a deceased child's special momentos. We lit a candle each day over the holidays and it added calmness and an opportunity to reflect on happier memories. Our family formed an outdoor prayer circle as we sent up balloons on Christmas day. I wore an angel pin on my shoulder for years after Mike left. It always felt as if he were with me. Another way to keep our youth's memories alive is starting a scholarship fund. Each year, I buy a meaningful Christmas ornament.

I would stare out at the lake or the sky and ask Mike a question. In less than 2 seconds, I would feel or imagine his immediate response. Was it wishful thinking, or was I really receiving the mysterious impulses that some believers feel are true communications from the spirit world.

I often wondered if it was easier or more difficult for parents who lost a very young child. Each new bit of knowledge and understanding about the mystery of Mike's death, inch by inch, brought me closer to a healing strength.

Sometimes I rationalized that there are worse ways to lose a child. How could I have lived with choking anger if a drunk driver or a sniper's bullet killed my child and got away uncaught? But what point is there in analyzing the degrees of such tragedy? Losing a baby, a youth, or an adult child is still unnatural in the sequence of life.

In grieving, besides denial, there is angering loss in just answering people who ask if you have children and how many. Do you just include your deceased to avoid the truth and then the painful explanation?

Sisters and brothers are in great distress when they can no longer say they have a brother or a sister. My girls loved saying they had both. Siblings thrive on happy parents. Now they suddenly have to deal with an abnormal family; immeasurably hurt parents, and worries of what is going to happen to the family in the future.

Siblings who lose one to suicide without ever knowing how disturbed their brother or sister really was feel how unfair it was to be left with such hurt when it didn't have to happen. They are also scared of their future for fear their own children could be lost the same way.

When our son died in September, our daughter's birthday was just 12 days away. It took her twenty years to tell me that she hated the month of her birthday because Mike ruined her life when he died.

Sadly enough, one child's death makes the parents paranoid about losing another. I called my daughters and checked on them constantly even though they were now in their forties. You pray every night that nothing happens to those you have left, or their children. It can be smothering and alienating.

When the family all leave you and you are alone with your grief, you often just sit quietly and begin remembering some memories. When I felt I had regained my sanity, I tried to concentrate on the wonderful opportunity of having raised a boy and two girls to be able to understand the similarities and the differences and the joy of rearing each sex.

One very important point for those who have never lost a child; never, never tell the bereaved to "Get Over It," or "Get on with Your Life." First of all, you don't know what you are talking about. You inflict much hurt and damage to the grief stricken who are already mired in so much pain. It's much like saying, "Oh well, he's gone and you can't do anything about it, so get on down the road."

Only a mother and father who have lost their child know that there is NO GETTING OVER IT for the rest of their entire life. Being a good listener is the single most important thing a friend or family member can do.

Strength Beyond Belief

I ponder just what life's about; the ups and downs so real
I wonder why the hard times; fall on loving ones who feel.
The special ones who really care; are always in the wings
Waiting just to give you hugs; and bring you loving things.
Oh God why is it we who care are given so much grief?
Or is it that you gave us strength to last beyond belief?
I wonder as I age so fast; what am I meant to do?
I feel that you've entrusted me; to send your message through
I'm ready God for life anew; on earth or up on high
I know I've done the best I could; I'm not afraid to die.

January 1998
I Love You Mike,
Mom

CHAPTER SEVEN

ᔕᔕ

ROAD TO RECOVERY

WHEN I BEGAN writing in my journal, it was strictly to transfer the pain to paper; to scream the unreal so I wouldn't have to scare all the people who kept asking questions and have to console them. I think I had to see it to believe it. I was compelled to pour out my trauma knowing I had a sick and crazy mind.

The death of my son turned my life totally upside down. It forever was going to change his future and ours and I didn't have the capacity to make sense of the shocking image of his face of death. I ran from it but it has never dissipated. I wrote to open doors to explanations, motivations, theories, strategies, descriptions, biblical views, and ways to live one day at a time.

Overwhelming idiocy slowly settled down to understandable jargon, suggestions for survival and truths learned by others that brought me closer to a sense of reality. Studying from books about depression, generalized anxiety and suicide opened my eyes to a subject on which I had never dealt. The books helped me to learn how brain chemistry works when the brain is healthy. It also explained how the breakdown of certain functions of the brain leads to a series of misperceptions, resulting in a downward spiral of exhausting thoughts of death and then peace.

I ended my journal after about six years. In 2000, I closed it but couldn't imagine just forgetting about all that I had learned. I had thought a lot about sharing the information with everyone who fell into the category of a parent mired in hell after losing a child to suicide; kids contemplating ending their own life; a friend seeing a sudden change in a close buddy; a sibling keeping silent; a teacher who recognizes a couple of signs which reoccur; a coach who doesn't realize how sensitive some of his team is; a clergyman who deals with depressed kids or does he?

I envision symptoms and risks of depression, anxiety and suicide on poster boards placed prominently in homes, schools, locker rooms, church classes, physician's offices, mental illness counselor's offices, and anywhere the public is sitting, waiting or passing by. If only these mental disturbances had been recognized, publicized and funded in the 90's, I feel certain I would have known his problems were much more than worrisome. I wouldn't have asked him when he had turned into such a worrywart. He conveyed most of the telltale signs and for more than two weeks; that's today's clear message.

Guilt was not a big part of our recovery but only because we knew nothing about mental illnesses since the subject was pretty hush-hush. Now I am obsessed with sharing every bit of lifesaving information for loving, in-tune parents who feel they are on top of everything with their kids.

Kids are secretly helpless and hopeless; they don't want to burden you! Isn't that unbelievably, innocently disastrous? And Fatal? Don't let this happen in today's world. Let every aspect of a bad moment, bad day, bullying, breakup, humiliation, disappointment, loss of a friend, be the opportunity to ask questions, show concern and point out the other side of these events in a positive way. Acknowledge the problem and ask what they think about ways to solve it.

Remind them a different outcome is just a day away. That nothing stays the same. Offer a story where you were so low, and what happened to turn it around. Listen to your kids. Show them the signs of mental problems, discuss suicide with questions requiring more than a yes and no. Don't overpressure and don't rave over your kids looks. Teach your kids that in order to succeed, they must fail as well. Teach them how to cope and be resilient. Constantly praising your child actually disables him. He or she will learn reliance if you back off and let them make decisions as much as possible, and don't make excuses for them. Play down materialistic importance.

Quietly praise their actions; their loyalty; their kindness, their care. Share your pride in them for working hard for grades, for wanting to practice for sports, for team success, for their assistance around the house, their overall attitude about things, their work ethic if employed and whatever else you see them do that prompts you to impart love and appreciation.

I was diagnosed with breast cancer in 2003 and after a year of treatment and surgeries, I revisited my manuscript for the second time and received helpful, but rejecting letters from literary agents to whom I sent query.

I wrote for the Hood County News, our local newspaper and put my manuscript aside once again for five years. After that experience, I took up oil painting purely by accident and loved it so much that I painted all day, practically every day. Now, picking up my manuscript for the third rewrite, I have been contacted by a large publishing company and we are going forward to share an alarming, devastating and preventable way of death.

Reading that 22 soldiers are killing themselves per day hurts me so much. Seeing high school girls making pacts to kill themselves on the same day enrages me. Feeling the pain of a family I read about who lost their son or daughter to suicide just drives me to alert people and further awareness. Suicide is preventable. Suicide doesn't have to happen. Education starts at home and then the value of life should be hammered into kids heads at school. Full disclosure of depression, anxiety and suicide will contribute to changing the rising statistics of needless deaths.

I read an interesting statement. Talk with children—not at them. Don't fill them with advice. Even to your sullen teenager a soft comment like, "I'm concerned about you, because you are so silent." Why are you so angry with me? Please let's work on this." What has happened in school lately that seems to have become a problem with you?" What is it about life that you love the most? What do you dislike the most in our family? Where do you see yourself in three years? What is it about your girlfriend that you like the most?" And so on....

As I healed, I kept asking God what I was supposed to learn from Mike's death. Year after year I pondered. And then the answer was blaring at me. His letter of goodbye told me he no longer had a sense of direction and purpose. After so many years of writing, of course it finally hit me that I had one direction in which to go; with three important purposes to accomplish. Save helpless kids; Help devastated parents; Honor our son, Mike, giving meaning to his life and his death.

Mike's anguish began when we learned that none of the three universities to whom Mike applied, six months earlier, had ever received his transcripts from his Alabama college administration office. We called and were informed that his baseball coach had failed to release Mike's scholarship money, so they were unable to forward his last semester's transcripts.

It took three weeks of no return calls from the angry coach who was unhappy that Mike was transferring. Finally, when we called the dean in charge of finances; the unused funds immediately got sent to the Administration office; but it is now July. By the time Mike got home, there were no baseball team openings to connect with.

After a month, Mike was falling to pieces without the routine he had been on since he was age 6. Not hearing a word from any of the three universities to whom he had sent his applications in February, and worrying whether he would lose credits in the transfer began to eat at him. He interned at our local hospital and started a lawn mowing business. He was also taking 12 credits at junior college in case he lost credits. My quiet boy stayed in his room a lot to study, but about every three hours we would walk around the block trying to pound his worries into the concrete under our feet.

As I write this it's totally unbelievable that we didn't realize he was in a death spiral from the fear and confusion screwing up his otherwise very smart brain. Dear God, did you need him back so badly?

The day we buried our son, the mail came. Mike was accepted as a senior at two universities. A refund also came from his junior college. He had quit the first week of September. He pretended he was going to school. He pretended he was studying in his room. He was planning his death. And we were in our office; in the room next door, doing our job. How could this be? How could this be?

I very much hope that my story and information on mental illnesses, anxiety, depression, and suicide helps families keep their children alive. Watch, listen, communicate and get help; four top priorities to save your kids.

"God protects the brokenhearted and brings them back home."
—*Billy Graham*

CHAPTER EIGHT

━━━━━ ❧ ━━━━━

ANXIETY

ACCORDING TO THE National Institute of Mental Health, there are several different varieties. GAD refers to generalized anxiety disorder; OCD identifies as obsessive-compulsive disorder; panic disorder; PTSD is post-traumatic stress disorder and social phobia is social anxiety disorder. Everyone reacts to stress with some anxiety, however, when it becomes extremely excessive, it is often difficult to control. Anxieties are the most common mental disorders in our country, and when out of control often lead to suicide.

Scientists, through imaging technology and neurochemical studies, say that the amygdala, which is an almond-shaped structure deep within the brain, appears to be the communication hub that processes incoming sensory signals and the parts that interpret the signals. It alerts the rest of the brain that is being threatened and triggers a fear or anxiety response. Emotional memories are stored in the central portion of the amygdala.

The hippocampus is the part of the brain that encodes threatening events into memories. Its size reduces according to the amount suffered in traumatic events, such as those in military combat or victims of abuse. Additionally, neurotransmitters, such as dopamine, serotonin and others have a job to do in transmitting alerts with accuracy. As science continues to uncover some of the mysteries of the brain, drugs are being developed that will reduce or block fear responses. Science is also developing ways to know how the brain generates new cells during our lifecycle. Stimulating growth of new neurons in the hippocampus may help sufferers of PTSD.

General Anxiety Disorder Symptoms:
Excessive ever-present worry
Tiring easily
Trouble concentrating
Irritability
Muscle tension
Sleep problems

Anxiety disorders occur along with mental or physical illnesses, including alcohol or substance abuse, which could easily mask anxiety symptoms. Perhaps as many as 50 million American adults are filled with fearfulness and uncertainty. And if these disturbances exceed six months, suicidal thoughts and sometimes actions take place. Often anxiety disorders pair with depression and that may mask the risk of suicide.

People with generalized anxiety disorder experience great tension and worry, expecting the worst even though there is no reason for concern. They are scared of money matters, health, family, school, work, relationships and are convinced about a disaster ahead. Even getting through a day seems to be beyond their control.

As told on Psych Central, the anxiety is so intense, it borders on irrational. In addition to the overpowering mental agony, generalized anxiety disorder may also bring on physical symptoms. Some of the symptoms include twitching, muscle tension, sweating, lightheadedness, trembling, headaches and irritability.

GAD usually comes on gradually and most often occurs in childhood, adolescence and young adults. It seems to be more common in girls or women than in boys and men. Excessive worry and apprehensive expectations for around 4-6 months and beyond strongly suggest seeing a mental health professional.

Severe anxiety can make a person unable to get through the easiest functions. This disorder may be brought on because of a biological factor, family background or extremely stressful life experiences. Other factors of mental illnesses being investigated are environmental conditions such as pollution, physical and psychological stress and even diet. Generic studies are exposing more and more valuable information which will contribute to understanding and treating mental illnesses and suicide.

A doctor will determine a diagnosis after evaluating whether a person's anxiety disorder is caused by a single or paired combination such as depression or alcohol/substance. Treatment is determined by the problem and the person's preference. One treatment method is medication with effective dosage, appropriate length of time and no apparent side effects. Anti-anxiety, antidepressants and beta-blockers are for control, never a cure.

Psychotherapy involves talking with a trained mental health professional, such as a psychiatrist, psychologist, social worker or counselor to learn what caused the anxiety disorder and how to deal with it. Cognitive-behavior therapy also helps treat anxiety disorders. The cognitive part helps to change the thinking pattern that supports their fears, and the behavioral part helps to change the way they react to anxiety provoking situations. Other methods that anxiety prone people may benefit from is to join a self-help or support group where they can share their problems. Internet chat rooms may be helpful but shouldn't be construed as reliable advice because it is coming from a stranger.

Meditation, exercise and stress management all help to lessen anxiety along with family support, but family unfortunately may trivialize the disorder to a stage, an age, hormones, attention or drama. Without medical help from a professional, suicide may be the end of the road and the only way a victim sees peace without pain.

A mental health specialist or counselor should also be contacted if you or your child, adolescent or young adult suffers from or is embarrassed by other type of anxiety disorders, such as social phobia, obsessive compulsive disorder, separation anxiety disorder, weight problem as in Anorexia Nervosa, hypochondriasis, or posttraumatic stress disorder.

One in five teens and young adults live with a mental health condition. The LBGTQ community, age 14-24, suffers the leading cause of suicide, because they have dual stress, particularly if their parents reject them.

LBGTQ individuals may face depression, PTSD, anxiety, and substance abuse. The National Alliance on Mental Illness strongly urges those suffering mental health illnesses due to secrecy, discrimination, bullying, rejection, and lack of support, get immediate help and intervention.

The Pride Institute (http://pride-institute.com/programs/lgbt-treatment) is a facility that offers a residential treatment program, which includes psychiatric care.

The Trevor Project (http://www.thetrevorproject.org/) is a support network for LBGTQ youth, providing crisis intervention and suicide prevention.

Fully sharing feelings
With a genuinely caring person
Makes the burden only half as heavy
Because it is now borne
By two people
—Abraham Schmitt

CHAPTER NINE

DEPRESSION

DEPRESSION IS A medical illness; just like a physical illness is a medical illness. Among the various degrees of depression is major or clinical depression, which is far more serious than a day or two of being sad. Major depression is depicted by overwhelming sadness. Symptoms suffered include pain, fear, rage, anxiety, lack of control and lack of understanding, helplessness and hopelessness.

Young people suffering from profound depression often lack the ability of seeking help and hide their problems and symptoms so as not to burden their parents. This crippling secret hides overwhelming pain, which then can become an obsession to rid themselves of pain, seek peace and end their life.

This brain disorder convinces its victims that they are worthless, hopeless and so exhausted, life isn't worth all the effort. They may cut out their social life, withdraw from activities they loved prior to their depression, and stay in their room to try to catch up on sleep that has alluded them and questions from their parents who have probably noticed that they don't seem themselves.

According to several mental health professionals, major or clinical depression appears to be a biologically based brain disease and is probably due to genetics or a malfunction in brain chemistry. It can develop at any age and displays differently in each individual.

The worst part of major depression is that the outward behavior of the profoundly depressed person often seems perfectly normal, other than a mood swing or bit of irritability now and then. Worry is often typical of teenagers simply because they have no experience in what's ahead. It does not present bizarre behavior, delusions or hallucinations, so is often unseen and unheard because it doesn't appear to be life threatening. Sadly enough, fifty percent of untreated clinical depression sufferers attempt or commit suicide.

Major depression can derive from a series of personal disappointments and life transforming events, or may be brought on by a single psychological trauma in a young person's life. Unrecognized and untreated, it may occur with greater seriousness or turn into profound sadness, mostly hidden from parents or friends. Depressed young people are also adept at passing off their behavior with another excuse.

Since depression can be defined as a biological vulnerability, it often surfaces when an alarming and disturbing life experience occurs. This vulnerability suggests that the condition may lie in the family's history. Often genes in a particular chromosomal region differ completely from the genes of people who do not have depression.

At the cellular level, depression has biochemical roots that alter the workings of nerve cells in the brain. Profoundly depressed people have unusual levels of one hormone, called cortisol. Several brain chemicals, namely neurotransmitters, serotonin, norepinephrine and dopamine can also have unusual levels that may have been inherited.

When chemical dysfunctions occur, imbalanced messengers, which transmit electrical signals between brain growth from age three to fifteen indicate a tangle of nerve cells growing in the area above the eyes, called the prefrontal cortex. When puberty ends, about half of those fibers prune away in order to create an effective network of circuits.

The prefrontal cortex is the center of executive functions; planning, organizing, impulse inhibition, goal setting and priority setting. If the development in this part of the brain is impaired, missing or slow to fully grow, catastrophic behavior may ensue. During this development period, risk taking may not be correctly assessed, indicating why so many teenagers do such seemingly ridiculous and dangerous and life-threatening things.

According to national mental health surveys, women and girls suffer depression twice as frequently as males. This frequency can be attributed to all the outside influences females experience, from hormonal effects of menstrual cycles, pregnancy, childbirth, infertility plus contraceptives. Women also experience much deeper feelings of losses and depression hits vulnerability. A survey also indicates that 37% of depressed women suffered physical or sexual abuse in their childhood.

Boys and men seem to be known for characteristics of, "Don't want to go there; don't want to talk about it." This is the reason they often suffer, "hidden depression." They can't express their fear or their feelings as they think it shows weakness. Emotional pain tends to make guys ashamed. Keeping so much inside, many turn to alcoholism or substance abuse or anti-social behavior.

Unfulfilled expectations cause males to suffer frustration, loss of self-esteem and great disappointment. On the other end, youth who achieve outstanding success in sports, grades and popularity, are often under great pressure and when things change, circumstances trigger depression and a complete mood altering.

Teens and young adults experiencing hormonal changes are trying to adjust to all the new social roles, new relationships, changes in their bodies, making decisions and trying to become their own person. If outside influences occur, they have an even harder life to deal with such as divorce, relocation, parent substance abuse, alcoholism, domestic abuse or sexual abuse. If they feel isolated, they become extremely depressed and are at high risk for suicide.

Depression brings on feelings of helplessness. Inadequate sleep, loss of interest in activities, indecisiveness, anxiety, fatigue and constant worry suddenly takes the depressed sufferer into a downward spiral of school grades and personal health. Perspective gets all out of whack and sadness doesn't go away. Suddenly everything is in great turmoil. Perception is completely distorted and results of anything tried all seem to go wrong, indicating that nothing is worth trying. Everything in life is hopeless. Suicide now ranks high for finding peace without pain.

When anxiety accompanies depression, a youth is more debilitated than ever. Isolation, silence, quitting, behaviors that don't make sense and total inability to bounce back after disappointment strongly indicate a youth suffering something very wrong. Youth between nine and seventeen who suffer the crippling dual of anxiety and depression present a serious and crucial mental health problem, often ending in suicide.

True statistics of youth completing suicide have never been reliable because the huge stigma against suicide prevents many parents from divulging their youth's mental dysfunction. Awareness helps prevention!

A study in 2014 determined that a blood test became the first objective scientific way to diagnose major depression, at least in adults. Perhaps by now the study has gone on to find more information regarding youth, but I could not find any recent and updated study information.

According to the WebMD, the test measured levels of nine genetic indicators, known as RNA markers in the blood, determining who may respond to cognitive behavioral therapy, which is the most common and effective treatment for depression. It could also determine how and if the therapy worked.

Just as in treating anxiety, depression treatment ranges from prescribed medication to evaluation by a psychiatrist or other mental health professionals. Clinical psychologists work with individuals and their families to understand the problems associated with depression. They are trained in counseling and psychotherapy. In addition, mental health counselors provide psychotherapy as well as human development and theory and group sessions. Community health centers provide information to people seeking help in mental health issues.

Paying attention to emotional well-being today is a bigger, more important issue than concentrating on physical issues. Seeking help for depression and anxiety is essential to save not just one life, but a classroom full of children, a plane full of passengers, a business with an angry ex-employee, a restaurant packed with happy diners, innocent automobile drivers on their way to somewhere, people enjoying jogging, and on and on in society these days. Total awareness of someone addicted to drugs and/or alcohol usually begins with a mental disorder and one who has slipped through the crack of awareness, concern, and sometimes life-saving assistance.

Today, parents, friends and siblings, instructors, coaches and faith professionals must believe and attend to assistance by paying detailed attention to an act, a comment, a change in personality or a call for help, realizing that a mental disorder is an injury or malfunction of the brain and its chemistry and vital to report to save lives.

If you have a feeling there is definitely something wrong with you, it's as simple as mentioning that to someone who cares about you. You are precious to so many people, even though you may feel that you are worthless to yourself. Talking about it and visiting a counselor of mental disorders is today's answer to stop severe depression and anxiety and prevent your suicide.

You have no idea that ending your problems and pain is horror for the person who finds you and those who care about you. You may take your pain away, but you have provided your family with a lifetime of pain. Know that you are going to drive your family crazy trying to untangle your dark secrets when all you had to do was get a professional to explain and treat your distress

SYMPTOMS OF SEVERE DEPRESSION

Persistent sadness or anxiousness and agitation
Feelings of worthlessness and helplessness
Excessive or inappropriate guilt
Constant expressions of worry
Excessive pessimism and self-criticism
Hopelessness about the future
Obsessing over school, work, sports or other subjects
Lack of emotion and inability to cry
Lack of personal hygiene or appropriate appearance
Secretiveness and withdrawal from family and friends
Loss of interest and pleasure in belongings and usual activities
Decreased energy and chronic fatigue
Involvement with drugs or alcohol
Poor memory and difficulty making decisions
"Everything is fine" explanation—Denial of true feelings
Difficulty concentrating
Irritability and restlessness
Loss of appetite and interest in food
Extreme overeating and weight gain
Difficulty in sleeping
Sleeping too much
Increased risk taking
Reoccurring thoughts of death, suicidal thoughts or action

Five or more of these symptoms, lasting over two weeks, may indicate severe depression and anxiety

———∿∿———

What lies behind us
and what lies before us
are tiny matters compared
to what lies within us.
—Ralph Waldo Emerson

———∿∿———

CHAPTER TEN

UNDERSTANDING AND COMMUNICATION OF MENTAL HEALTH WELL-BEING

"ONE IN FIVE Americans has a diagnosable mental health condition, and one half of all lifetime cases of mental illness begins by age 14." says Barbara Van Dahlen, Ph.D., Founder and President of *Give an Hour*, the backbone of the *Campaign to Change Direction*.

We all have mental health, and we all experience emotional pain and suffering during our lifetime. Every family has a story of a personal struggle whether it be a suicide, untreated postpartum depression, substance abuse, homelessness, criminality or schizophrenic behavior. Even though this is the case, most people fail to discuss it, get control over it with medical counseling, or refuse to accept it, totally ignoring it and hoping it will all go away.

At present, over $2.5 trillion is being spent on mental health disorders, and a projection of approximately $6 trillion will be spent by 2030. If we view mental illness equally as important if not more important than physical illness, with education and intervention, prevention would prevail.

More people die by suicide than in automobile accidents. And suicides among youth between age 10-24 and suicides among youth age 10-24 have tripled since 1950s. Twenty-two members of the military complete suicide every day. Fear and ignorance are at the core of resistance to change our beliefs and broadcast the reality without stigma and embarrassment. There are now over one hundred professional organizations, corporations, communities, academic institutions, non-profits and governmental agencies all working together to blast collective impact of changing the culture of mental health, mental illness and wellness. The focus of these bodies of people is to get America to learn the five signs of seeing and hearing someone suffering emotionally and needing our help by alerting their family, friends, workplace, school, sports coach or faith director. Think of it as saving a life.

Teaching us all to recognize and respond to the five signs of emotional suffering allows us to open up the conversation about mental health in classrooms, community centers and in our own home. If we, ourselves, pay attention to our own emotional well-being, just as we do about our physical well-being, we will realize the importance of getting help for our anxiety and depression and not be the least embarrassed.

Remember, our mental health needs a check-up just like our physical health. If we'd share stories about recognizing and improving our own mental health, as well as that of one in our family, the more open and acceptable the truth of the brain chemistry mishap will be understood and not something to be ashamed of.

Finally, there is a push to change the culture of mental health so that we can identify someone who is acting totally different, out of character, full of obvious anxiety, quitting activities once loved, looking unhealthy and unkempt day after day when that wasn't how they used to look, or so pessimistic and hopeless acting that you are prompted to share your thoughts with the sufferer or a family member or friend.

Many years ago, my daughter in college called to tell me her roommate was so despondent and distraught that she was afraid she might try to take her life. I called her mom and dad, they drove the 5 hours to her dorm, picked her up, brought her home, took her to a mental health professional and set up appointments to continue at her school. She improved, eventually married, had a child and lives a very successful life co-owning a small company.

You may be afraid you will lose a friend if you "rat" on him, but that is the very reason conversation needs to be held everywhere so that hard feelings have no part in positive help, because you may well have saved that friend's life. Just as we know the signs of a heart attack, we can learn and raise awareness of the signs of emotional suffering so that those in need receive the care and support they deserve.

You Could Have Fooled Me

I wish you hadn't gone away
I thought we had it all, you and me
I guess you fooled me!
What is it that you do in this new place of yours?
Peace and love surely keep you well
Otherwise, why did you leave us in this hell?
I am recovering
Because it's what you would have wanted me to do
You could have fooled me.
See me now?
Joy has found its way back!
You could have fooled me.
You were so deserving of the best
I pray God's love and peace
Now give you rest… .
I Love You so much. I'll miss you forever
—Mom
October 1997

CHAPTER ELEVEN

SUICIDE

SUICIDE SEEKS TO achieve two things; sought-after peace, an end to the exhausting pain, or both. The overwhelming and usually misconstrued hopelessness is the ending of a period of time where the emotional sufferer has misunderstood, formed misperceived attitude, tunnel-vision focus and inept conclusions about the present and the future. The victim of suicide becomes totally powerless over his own brain function, may be predisposed genetically, or may be abused by alcohol or drugs and not capable of making a rational decision.

Suicidal reasoning may be the result of a loss of a loved one, the loss of a past way of life, the loss of the idea you had of yourself because a goal hadn't been achieved or you hadn't fulfilled the destiny you once promised yourself. The failure of a dream you had most of your life is now suddenly unattainable, convincing you that you are worthless and life is hopeless.

The logic of suicide is totally chaotic. It's like being in a completely different dimension. When a person is suicidal and comes to the decision to end his life, he has entered a completely shut-off and convincing world, where if the letter hasn't arrived, the answers to questions are all wrong and future plans are totally screwed-up, these indicators take on special all-wrong meaning and contribute to the ending of everything.

Now, after the fact, I can see that Mike's downward spiral began with a series of personal disappointments. When he became aware that his goals were unattainable, depression must have silently crept in. As it intensified, actual pain began. Anxiety seemed to overtake each and every situation.

As Mike's thought process got more and more sluggish, so did his physical being. And so began the unhealthy thought process that never dealt with consequences. It only dealt with issues of how to get rid of pain.

Evidently, Mike's thoughts of the hopeless future must have taken over his unhealthy brain function and he probably never heard any of our ideas, advice, assurances and ways to turn everything around. He must not have felt all of our love and concern. The circle of death thoughts was well into his disintegrated mind. Suicide was to be completed.

When Mike became *himself, (in our ignorant determination)* a day or two before his death, we obviously misread his aura. He had entered what is termed the, "euphoric stage" of the death path of suicide. His calm, cheerful, normal acting behavior came solely because he had made his decision and worked out the way to end his life. During this stage, he had renewed energy. When the right day, the right time and the right method presented itself, the impulsive act of suicide was completed. Mike's tormented mind finally found peace.

For years, I was constantly amazed that none of us realized what Mike was going through. It wasn't as if he kept his turmoil to himself. We talked about it three and four times each day from June to mid-September. Had we been lucky enough to have seen posted signs of depression, I'm certain I would have associated Mike's symptoms and probably panicked that he showed ten signs of the 21 I've seen on the depression sign lists.

I knew the signs of cancer and heart attack, so why didn't I know the signs of depression? It wasn't publicized much before 1999, when the government got behind mental health awareness and appointed the Surgeon General to start a national campaign. Nineteen years later, the number of suicides is so elevated, but the automatic recognition of anxiety and depression is still lacking and the subject still stigmatized.

Technology is finally defining that depression can be inherited from family genes. It can be caused and furthered by alcohol and substance abuse, brought on by brain injury, bad learning experiences, brain chemistry interruption or transmitters chemically lacking.

Several conditions may predispose a youth to end his or her life. Among these are severe depression, violent temperament, romantic disconnection, debilitating or terminal illness, personal financial chaos, legal problems, job loss, grade drops, drug and alcohol dependence, mental and physical abuse and heredity. But the one common denominator of all of these conditions is that, prior to suicide, somewhere along the way, the person became depressed and worse, became anxiety ridden at the same time.

The moment a young person ends his life, he is in the moment of his most hopeless despair. He could be described as vulnerable, temporarily insane, angry and resentful, agitated and panicked, or just sad, scared and in too much pain.

Generally, no one is there to hear if there is an inner voice commanding his death. Usually, no one is around to see the sudden impulse. And we never really know how long our youth has suffered despair or tormenting pain. It could have been recent, it could have been some time ago, and it could have been for a lifetime. Silence is deadly. Ignorance, on our part, is deadlier.

There are many common similarities among those who attempt suicide. When asked, they all say their mental capacity was so distorted, they could not see the future in any way. The more they were surrounded with love, the more they realized how undeserving they were. They felt they were very selfish in thinking only about themselves. The more they worried about being a burden on those who loved them, the more they turned inward to find the way to end their misery and pain.

The sad thing about suicidal kids who make the attempt to kill themselves is that they don't seem to have the sense of feeling, like their thinking is paralyzed and they have no sense of control over daily management. They don't realize that suicide is the permanent way to end a temporary problem. This fact must be drilled into our kid's heads. Things change in a moment, a day, a week, a month or a year. They also need to be told that suicide is the worst possible death a family must endure.

Several stunning events may trigger suicide among those who are suffering depression. Some of those include the death of a family member or close friend; an assault, car accident or painful physical or emotional event; something particularly embarrassing that seems major to a young person; failing an important exam at school, or refusal of entrance to a college; being dropped from a team sport, or kicked out of school; when a best friend moves away; and continuous humiliation, degradation and abuse from school mates or family. Circumstances of suicide often continue to be a mystery, particularly when the death is a result of a drowning, single car accident, drug or alcohol overdose or an unidentified ingestion. Often those left behind do not report suicide accurately and conflicting opinions lack the evidence necessary to identify actual number of suicides.

According to the most recent official data released by the American Association of Suicide revised in December, 2015 with official final data, there were approximately 43,000 suicides nationally in 2014; breaking down to approximately 118 suicides per day. Of these numbers, young people 15—24 years of age completed suicide at the rate of 14 per day, or 5100 per year. In more detailed figures, about 1 young person dies by suicide every hour and a half.

Suicide among youth under 24 is the most serious American health problem today. It is the second leading cause of death in young people attending college. One in ten college students (many more if reported with accuracy) consider suicide, and draw up specific plans or actually attempt it.

For young people age 15 -24, suicide is the third leading cause of death and that exceeds homicide. Per the CDC, in March, 2018, the #1 cause of death in the age group of 10-14 is suicide; a 70% jump in 10 years.

The figures for nonfatal attempts exceeds one million, one hundred thousand, or an attempt every 30 seconds. Four times as many males complete suicide as females, but three times as many females attempt it. And for every suicide, 18 people are intimately and hurtfully affected. They are called suicide survivors, which, in my opinion, conflicts with the term suicide attempters who survived. To me, those who are left behind are often what I consider to be the victims of a completed suicide.

Per many suicide articles, only one in four persons who complete suicide leave a parting message. And when they do write a note with their last desperate thought, it usually is not typical of their outward behavior. Most of the letters have a casual tone, mentioning trivial reasons, rather than the real motives that have propelled the sufferer to end his life.

The letters often depict a great loss and zero faith in the future. The subject of depression or pain is rarely mentioned in suicide letters. In addition, the writer generally offers an apology for his last deed and wishes his loved ones well with the hope that they will see each other later in life. This is exactly what Mike's letter said.

DANGER SIGNS OF SUICIDE
Talking about killing yourself, even in joking around
Statements about hopelessness, helplessness, or worthlessness
Preoccupation with death
Loss of interest in things and activities always cared about
Visiting or calling people you've always cared about
Suddenly calmer and happier
Making arrangements, setting your affairs in order
Giving things away

In the past, the government has been hesitant to make this list available in the classroom because they felt it would promote suicide through the suggestion that suicidal thoughts and behaviors are normal responses to extreme stress. Now, the subject is headed in a direction with just the opposite approach. Awareness is the whole point. Having a conversation with our kids in the classroom and everywhere else is the immediate scream to kids from 10 up. And kids want us to be aware, to intervene and help them get through their hard times with total honesty.

Protection against suicide is the most important intervention we can accomplish. It includes positive resistance and support physically and mentally. When raising a child, teach him skills which allow him to solve his own problems, enabling him to acquire resilience and coping skills. This is urgent in order to support strength in adverse situations and allow your child to be able to bounce back after disappointments.

Restrict access to lethal methods of suicide. Obtain medical and mental health support for your child and support them in your family and community. Encourage them in your religious beliefs that suicide is not a permissible way to solve a problem. It's a permanent way to end a temporary problem. As our youth learn how to cope with stressful situations, they can look at the circumstances as a challenge and an opportunity for change instead of despair.

People need to realize that suicides can happen in all of our families. We must stop denying its existence. Suicide is almost exclusively due to depression and anxiety. Help identify depression now. As a family, what can we do to keep our children from falling into depression? We can encourage our children to share their disappointments as well as their joy. We can allow them to share their anger and distress. We can share their feelings and be supportive without demanding to know why and interrogating them.

If we can overcome our obstacles together, we will be instilling resilience and encouraging coping skills. Talking about feelings can add supportive emotional release and show that you respect your child's opinions. Intervening promptly when our youth is faced with a significant life event, such as a relationship breakup, court appearance, family split or rejection from a school, helps keep the stress level down. Bullying and humiliation in front of school mates is huge and must be shared at the start and put to a stop.

Suicide threats should always be taken seriously because threats usually equate to, "I can't handle things anymore." And expressions such as, "I'd be better off dead," or "I won't be a problem for you much longer," and "Nothing matters anymore," are often signs of a future attempt. When youth seem obsessed about a subject, don't even think of giving them advice or lectures. Instead, sit down and listen to what is on their minds. Tell them you are trying to understand them and ask what they could tell you to help you get it.

Misinterpretation is a result of distortion caused by incorrect chemical amounts being triggered, impulses sent to the wrong connectors, not enough serotonin or other malfunctions. Imagine that two people are looking at the same obstacle. One sees the obstacle as a path of stepping stones. The other sees it as a 90-foot wall. The first sees the path clearly and shows the second person the steps and the success of the journey. The second person doesn't believe a thing he's hearing and totally tunes him out.

The misperception in depression contributes to giving the sufferer a sense of reality that is really distorted. False impressions turn into realistic conclusions and those conclusions trigger what seems reasonable and that is to end the chaos and pain and seek peace.

Scientists can see brain chemistry malfunctions and are researching implanting a pacemaker to alter erroneous brain chemistry paths. All of this insight into the technology center of our brain will enable people to see that the brain's ill health isn't different than the malfunction of our heart, kidneys or liver.

Approximately 30% of suicides are due to self-poisoning or overdosing. Fifty percent of male suicides are committed by firearms. Hanging or jumping off of high structures comprise other methods of self-inflicted deaths. As a parent, you can remove firearms and monitor your personal medications; keep a close eye on consumption levels of your alcohol and watch your youth closely for signs of drug use.

According to "Healthy Children.org," suicide doesn't just happen. Recent studies show that 90% of teens who kill themselves have some type of mental health problem or mood disorder. Besides depression and anxiety, drug or alcohol abuse, others suffer from previous sexual or physical abuse, trouble with their sexual identity, loss of friends and bullying in school or over the internet.

A mood disorder is an illness of the brain, and it can come on suddenly or be present on and off during a person's lifetime. Thousands of teens in America commit suicide each year. It is the third leading cause of death for 15 to 24 years old. Most parents attribute teenage problems to just being a teenager. Being aware of all the obvious signs of depression, anxiety and drug/alcohol abuse and talking about it freely should totally negate suicides slipping through the cracks.

In the present, so many causes or combinations of causes call attention to the overwhelming numbers of depressed youth. The majority of causes are:

Drug abuse	Relationship breakup
Love loss	Loss of limb, blindness, deafness
Parent's divorce	Domestic violence or abuse
Parents unemployed	Lack of success academically
House financial problems	Dislike of school
Inept parenting	Being cheated on
Peer pressure	Emotional disorders or abuse
Bullying online and in school	Sexual abuse or rape
Social rejection	Mental disorders
Anger or guilt	Lack of parental interest

From Suicide.org, alarmingly, suicide is the second leading cause of death for college students, and the first cause of suicide for college students with untreated depression. With students being away from home, parents may be unaware unless they are fortunate to be alerted by their youth's friend or with whomever he may share his problems.

According to Florida State University psychologist, Roy Baumeister in his article, *"Suicide as Escape from Self,"* there are six primary steps in the escape theory, ending in a probable suicide when all the criteria are met. Having attempted suicide and recognizing his own suicidal ideation, Roy Baumeister tells his personal knowledge of being inside the suicidal mind.

STEP 1: FALLING SHORT OF STANDARD

Most people who kill themselves lived better-than-average lives. Suicide rates are higher in states with better weather, better quality of life, higher in society, and college students with higher grades because their parents presumably had higher expectations. Having had an idealistic lifestyle, unreasonable standards for personal happiness are created and particularly emotionally fragile youth don't know how to handle unexpected setbacks. When these setbacks keep continuing, these people of a more privileged and comfortable past seem to have a much harder time coping with failures. *This identifies with my son, Mike.*

STEP 2. ATTRIBUTES TO SELF

These people loathe themselves for the trouble they find themselves in. Self-blame or condemnation of self is prevalent in suicides. There is not a big problem with self-esteem, but rather the negative turn of events makes the sufferer guilty, shameful, or humiliated and they dislike themselves and feel there is no hope for change.

STEP 3. HIGH SELF-AWARENESS

People who had a happier past or a goal in mind, now find it impossible to achieve that goal, and they constantly compare themselves to the person they thought they would be. They're unforgiving of their present state with no chance of recovering their past self. The reality of their suicide letter of goodbye is usually in first-person, singular pronouns, which shows high self-awareness. They rarely refer to "us," or "we," because they are consumed with self in the scope of worthlessness and detachment. If mentioning a significant other, they refer to them as being cut off, distant or separate with no opposition or sense of understanding. *This also appeared in Mike's letter of goodbye.*

STEP 4. NEGATIVE AFFECT

Anxiety—also experienced as guilt, self-blame, ostracism, worry and social exclusion, is a common thread in most suicides. It also brings on acute shame. The most misperceived part of the shamed existence is that guilt seems to seek punishment. The acute anxiety also brings a loss of consciousness and accelerates a need to rid the pain. At this juncture, most suicidal people think in three ways to escape the painful self-awareness; drugs, sleep and death. Death is the only permanent fix.

STEP 5. COGNITIVE DECONSTRUCTION

The fifth step in the escape theory illustrates how seriously inaccessible the suicidal mind is from normal cognitive thinking. The outside world soon becomes a much simpler affair in our heads. Things get cognitively broken down into ever growing low-level and basic elements. The time perspective of suicidal people changes in a way that makes the present moment seem amazingly long; and that is because they have anxious awareness of the recent past and the future too, both of which they seek to escape from in a narrow unemotional focus at the moment. The suicidal sees the present as endless. The defense mechanism clicks in which helps the suicidal withdraw from the past and sends anxiety of an intolerable hopeless future.

Fake suicide letters often give specific instructions such as, "feed the cat." Real letters are mostly void of spiritual or deep thoughts. The goal is to forget the past, obliterate the future, become effectively present in a way to get out of the grief, worry and anxiety. And the thought of getting rid of all that pain and enter into peace is what brings a sense of calmness and a true feel-good essence because it is all almost over.

STEP 6. DISINHIBITION

The final mental stage separates suicidal ideation from the actual act of suicide. Behavioral ideology negates the suffering of loved ones left behind. This action disallows the inherent "wrongness" of suicide. In addition to suicidal desire, the person needs the acquired capability for suicide, which involves both a lowered fear of death and an increased physical pain tolerance. Suicide literally hurts.

When it comes to inherited variants of impulsivity, fearlessness and greater physical pain tolerance, the evidence of suicidal tendencies may be present. *Mike's dad took high risks in his life, having been born in Latvia, invaded by Russians, then escaping to Germany and in the presence of undetonated bombs and Han grenades, perhaps his risky traits transferred.*

Before his death, I learned that he bungee jumped and also burned his arm badly, telling me he ran into his friend's cigar. Never did it occur to me that my dear "worrywart" would ever in a million years think of taking his own life. It can happen to any of us. It happens to thousands of great kids.

To give comfort to families left behind, there are several gospel accounts attesting that God forgives all sins except blasphemy against the Holy Spirit. (Mark 3:28,29 Matthew 12:31, 32 Luke12:10) Survivors of suicide loss should know that their loved one is in the hands of a loving and gracious God who made provisions for the forgiveness of sins.

As we come out of the shock of losing our loved one to suicide, we need to look to God for the hope our youth lost and the purpose that will bring us back to the wholeness of living with meaning.

Gift from God

You've taught me well from way on high
I laugh and love and write and cry…
It took me years to get through this
Your voice, your face, I'll always miss…
You sent the babies one by one
It gave me hope; they make it fun…
I never dreamed that I'd find joy
But here I am, without my boy…
Your spirit lives, you're in my heart
Despite the fact that we're apart…
I wear an angel at my breast
And having had you, I can rest…
Time and faith and my love, Rod
All serve to heal me; Gift from God…

I love you. Mom
March, 2003

CHAPTER TWELVE

REALIZATION AND RECONSIDERATION

TO BEGIN WITH, as we raise our children, resilience, coping, "getting it," is the key to positivity, self-reliance, self-esteem, and the "end-all," "be-all," answer to keeping our children from being the victims of depression and anxiety.

Resilience can be taught through simple everyday experiences. The simplest lesson is to just let them have to wait patiently in the car during a traffic jam or in a restaurant when it's crowded. We don't have to provide them with entertainment. Let them decide on their own how to contain impatience.

Give your child independence to try new things that they initiate, such as opening a container that is difficult for them. Encourage them to continue trying until they succeed. This may seem insignificant, but it's huge in reality. If you do it for them each time, they will always expect help from you or others.

Encourage your child to make their decision to eat healthy foods rather than junk food. Skip junk food even 6 nights a week and substitute something tasty instead of French fries, lettuce wraps instead of bread.

Do not give your kids every single item they want. Especially when everyone else has it. Saying no teaches them to cope with distress and disappointment or perhaps makes them decide to earn the thing they so want by doing chores, help for a neighbor, or other extra accomplishments.

Set aside a few times a year to have your children pick out some of their things to give away to children less fortunate. This gives them excellent opportunities to think about the ability to give and not just take. It teaches them how to make happiness for others by giving.

Give your youth an opportunity to help younger children in simple ways by reading to them, swinging them on the playground, showing them how to care for an animal and any number of life's lessons. They will realize their importance to others and develop a sense of self-awareness.

Teach your children to look at struggles as challenges to overcome. Ask them to think about the different ways they could overcome their problem. Let them do the decision making. We rush to their aid, making it all too easy. Let them know that every challenge only serves to make them stronger and that will give them the idea that stronger is better; that there are choices they can make on their own.

Encourage your children to maintain a positive attitude about chores or homework by giving them a sense of creativity or fun like setting a timer to show them how easy it is to help around the house in a much quicker way than they thought. Keeping a positive outlook makes whatever effort your child puts in he feels he did the best he could. If he thinks negatively, nothing will either look right or feel right.

One of the most riveting stories I read while on the search for why our son took his own life, was written by Viktor Frankl, Prisoner #119104, a Jewish neurologist and psychologist, arrested in 1942, and held with his wife and parents in a Nazi concentration camp.

Three years later, his camp was liberated. His pregnant wife and most of his family had died. He lived. He wrote a book entitled "Man's Search for Meaning," in nine days. It turned out to be a best seller. Frankl saw in the camps that those who found meaning even in the tragedies of death had more resilience to suffering through the worst circumstances.

He wrote, "Everything can be taken from a man but one thing; the human freedom of choosing one's own way to choose one's attitude. The suicidal inmates he counseled with suffered from hopelessness with nothing to live for. To keep them alive, he convinced them that life expected something from them. He gave meaning to their existence.

Once they determined they had a responsibility toward another human being and that they had unfinished work to do, they released the thought of ending their life. Once they were convinced of why they were on earth, they could bear almost anything.

Even though millions of copies of his book were sold worldwide, and he was deemed one of ten most influential authors in the United States, our country seemed to be and still is more interested in the pursuit of individual happiness rather than the search for meaning.

Happiness without meaning characterizes self-absorption. Happiness cannot be pursued-it must be as a result of the search for meaning. Having read Mike's letter of goodbye and shockingly learning that he no longer felt he had direction or a sense of purpose, I was sent into an unknown way of life.

My compelling goal was the driving obsession to learn, convince and scream urgency to parents and kids everywhere that total awareness of anxiety and depression is life saving. From that awareness, meaning, resilience, direction and purpose are possible for the helpless and hopeless youths and for those left behind, because they didn't read the signs and get immediate help.

Frankl's biggest contribution was establishing suicide prevention centers for teenagers to have open conversations with a therapist to overcome depression and achieve peace through finding their unique meaning in life. A meaningful life uses your strength and talent to serve others. It is a love of giving regardless of sacrifices, negative results or exhausting stress.

Research shows that having meaning and purpose in life enhances mental and physical health, increasing well-being, self-esteem and resiliency, decreasing the chances of depression. The search for and the recognition of meaning is what brings acceptance of happiness. And happiness is attained when we receive benefit from it.

The most compelling new research about resilience focuses on mindfulness, which enables your brain to concentrate on the present. Mindfulness actually can be identified in brain research. The reward of this trait is that it is particularly helpful in exhibiting less emotional reactivity to a stressful situation

Resilience is our ability to adapt well and recover quickly after stress, adversity, trauma, or tragedy. A resilient disposition enables you to be able to maintain poise and a healthy level of physical and psychological wellness in the face of life's challenges.

If you are less resilient, you are more likely to dwell on problems, feel overwhelmed, use unhealthy coping tactics to handle stress, and develop anxiety and depression. You need to train your attention so that you're more intentional about your perception. If you use purposeful, trained attention to decrease the negative thoughts in your mind, you can bring greater focus on the most meaningful aspect of an experience.

Programs incorporating these approaches can improve your resiliency, enhance your quality of life, and decrease your stress and anxiety.

Meditation is also a huge help in dealing with stress. This activity shows in brain imaging and continues to ease stress when meditation is over. It transforms our baseline and a solid baseline is valuable when the going gets tough.

ADDITIONAL TIPS TO BUILD RESILIENCE IN CHILDREN, YOUTH AND ADULTS INCLUDE:

Developing a core set of beliefs that nothing can shake
Find meaning in whatever stressful or traumatic thing happens
Try to keep a positive outlook
Take cues from someone you know who is especially resilient
Don't run from things that scare you—face them squarely
Be quick to reach out for support when things go all wrong
Learn new things as often as you can
Find an exercise regimen you'll stick with
Don't beat yourself up or dwell on the past
Recognize what makes you uniquely strong- and own it.

Today's realization is that kids are killing themselves because mental illness, whether brief, or prolonged, inborn or acquired, has been swept under the rug, overlooked, under-funded, misunderstood, uninsured, and kept secret for many years, and that mental illness is as important, if not more important, than physical health and crying for recognition as a national health problem that demands full awareness, intervention and extinction.

Post the lists of anxiety and depression everywhere including church, school, home, work offices, wherever people are sitting and could pay attention, possibly alerting them to their own child, youth or young adult.

Undetected, unmedicated and unmitigated, depression is the closest step to suicide for many. To stop this, we simply have to see it, hear it and stop it with immediate help.

THESE URGENT FACTS NEED TO BE KNOWN TO HELP SO MANY:

Recognize an alarming cry for help through awareness of the signs of depression and anxiety
Understand that talking about suicide does not cause someone to

be suicidal.

Over 43,000 Americans kill themselves yearly.

The number of attempts is much greater, but accurate information is often withheld

Suicide is the second leading cause of death among young people ages 15-24

Suicide is the tenth cause of death among all age persons

Almost 4 males kill themselves compared to women

Suicide occurs across all age, economic, social and ethnic boundaries

Firearms are the most common tool used among young or elderly white males

Survivors left behind may be subject to suicide and emotional problems

WAYS TO ASSIST SOMEONE THREATENING SUICIDE:

Learn the warning signs of anxiety and depression

Get involved, show interest and support

Ask the person if he or she is thinking about suicide

Be direct and talk openly and freely about suicide

Listen to expression of feelings; and accept the feelings

Be non-judgmental. Do not lecture or give advice on the value of life

Don't dare the person to do it

Don't advise to behave differently

Don't ask why for it encourages defensiveness

Offer empathy, not sympathy

Don't act shocked -it encourages distance

Don't be sworn to secrecy. Seek support

Offer hope that there are alternatives

Take action. Remove suicidal means if possible. Get help from suicide support prevention agencies

Be aware of feelings, thoughts and behaviors

Millions of Americans momentarily think about suicide at one point in their life. But people in the midst of a crisis often perceive their problem as inescapable and feel total loss of control. Their common daily thoughts include:

Can't make decisions; can't see any way out; Don't feel worthwhile or in control; Can't eat, sleep or work. Can't get someone's attention.

Talk to Someone; Contact:

A school support group (if provided)
A community mental health agency
A school counselor or psychologist
A suicide prevention/crisis intervention center
A private therapist
A family physician
A religious/spiritual leader

In reconsideration of the increase in known suicides once again, a collective impact effort designed to change the culture of mental health in America emerged to create a common language by educating all Americans about the five key signs of emotional suffering.

The national effort, launched by founder, Dr. Barbara Van Dahlen, a clinical psychologist and president of Give an Hour, its backbone organization, on March 4, 2015. The Campaign to Change Direction was presented to 400 politicians, the First Lady, Michelle Obama, business leaders and mental health advocates on May 23, 2016, in Concord, New Hampshire. The event focused on bringing into open discussion common ways to recognize mental distress. The 5 key signs of mental suffering are identified as:

Personality Change—Not seeming like yourself for a prolonged period

Agitation—Unusually anxious, edgy or irritable

Withdrawal—Normally outgoing-now suddenly withdrawn, remote or isolated

Poor Self Care—Decrease in hygiene, drinking or abusing drugs

Helplessness—Overwhelmed by life. Expressions of grief, guilt or worthlessness

Teaching the five signs of emotional suffering can only help if the whole judgmental attitude of mental illness changes. It is to be reminded at all times that it is a disease of the brain, just like a disease of the liver, kidneys or stomach. Open discussion of anxiety, depression, suicide and mental illness in general will eventually help millions just by ridding the world of the stigmas attached to mental illnesses.

To understand the terminology regarding suicide we need to identify the various levels: Suicide means killing oneself. The act pertains to a person willingly, or ambivalently, taking his or her own life. This behavior falls within the self-destructive spectrum.

A completed suicide means that the person died. A successful suicide is not appropriate as the goal is to prevent suicide and provide treatment.

A suicide attempt involves a serious act, as in a fatal dose of medication and being found by accident. Without the person being discovered, the individual would be dead.

A suicide gesture indicates a cry for help, not a gesture of permanency.

A suicide gamble is when patients gamble their lives that they will be found in time and the person who discovers them save their life. Such as a youth ingesting a fatal dose of drugs, feeling sure a family member will be home before death occurs.

A suicide equivalent involves a situation in which the person does not attempt suicide. Instead, he uses behavior to get some of the reactions that suicide would have caused. Running away from home, wanting to see how her parents respond. Are they sorry for their treatment of her? This is an indirect cry for help.

Suicide ideation. The ideas or mind set of possibly engaging in suicide.

One in five Americans has a diagnosable mental health condition, and one half of lifetime cases of mental illness begin by age 14, according to The American Association of Suicidology. The biggest problem is that so many are reluctant to discuss their own mental problems, let alone that of their youths, they don't even recognize that they themselves need help.

Just as you should now be required to listen to someone who is acting very differently, drinking excessively and talking threateningly, you should also know to never criticize, make a judgment or threaten to tell someone else without their permission.

Dealing with survivors of suicide, you also need to know the way to listen to them with compassion regardless of your discomfort. If they wish to share their story with you, let them speak at their own pace, be patient and offer empathy. Repetition is a part of their healing so if you hear the same story multiple times, just understand they find that necessary.

All a person left behind is looking for is your presence and your conditional listening. Don't say you know how they feel unless you have lost a son or daughter, mother or father, sister or brother, grandmother or grandfather and can totally relate if you feel deeply for the survivor.

But I will see you again
And your heart will rejoice
And your joy no one will take from you.
-John 16:22

CHAPTER THIRTEEN

PREVENTION

SUDDENLY, IN 1999, the United States Department of Health and Human Services realized that suicide was a serious public health problem. Along with the World Health Organization (WHO), Centers for Disease Control and Prevention (CDC), and SPAN (Suicide Prevention Advocacy Network), among others, including an organization made up of suicide survivors (persons left behind) attempters of suicide, community activists and mental health clinicians, joint effort sponsored a national conference on suicide prevention. The Surgeon General issued a Call to Action (AIM) Awareness, Intervention and Methodology, which served as the framework for the prevention of suicide.

At that particular time, suicide was the eighth leading cause of all deaths, and there were suicides completed every 17 minutes. Now that number is every 12 minutes. Every single group, community, committee, corporation and individual who tried to scream awareness and intervention meant it with all their heart.

The only problem was that people were keeping their personal thoughts secret. They were not seeking help from friends, their parents, their church, their school, a mental health clinic or admitting they even had a problem in their head. The stigma of suicide was overpowering. It still is. But telling our stories, coming out with total honesty and acknowledging depression is opening up a conversation so badly needed

First of all, believe that suicide and depression are national problems. Mental health is not given the respect, acknowledgment, or understanding as physical health is. And it's actually far more important in terms of the number of those dying by their own hand, or the killing of others for no apparent reason. In ten years, the number of mass murders can attest to the urgent need for recognition of mental disorders. Warning signs of a mental disorder can be seen or heard clearly if you are looking and listening, checking health alerts, informing someone of your awareness to be followed up by another and another until mental health professionals are included.

Realize how devastating it is for a student to be bullied, pushed around, humiliated, scared, feel worthless or hopeless because of YOU! Would you ever take a gun and deliberately shoot someone in the head? Because if you are or have a bully in your family or as a friend, you too are responsible for a youth's death.

If you are the coach, principal, or teacher of a bully and see a student going downhill fast and don't acknowledge the urgent problem in front of you, you too can consider yourself responsible for his death.

Never underestimate the power of your actions. With one gesture, with one personal commitment to a person, either bully or victim, you must think about it as your duty to change a person's life. You must feel it essential to make an impact on another's life. That's what we must do to give care, love and life.

Having spent years of suffering, years of writing my ever-constant pain, years of trying to find acceptance, it is now completely impossible and irresponsible not to try to convince you, or your youth to pinpoint two or three signs of depression and anxiety, probe with a few questions about the obviousness, the feelings of the past and the future, and the assurance that you will provide them with immediate assistance from a professional counselor.

Even though it may not ever occur to you that your children or friends would ever take their own life, you must stop being that vulnerable. You must realize that your kids or friends hide things from you many times to keep you from freaking out or thinking that you don't have a clue about them, or thinking you don't give a flip about them. Their minds just aren't at all in sync with yours. They are not thinking clearly. Everything seems to be distorted if they are experiencing mental disorders, whether recent or long time.

When discussing prevention of suicide, it takes complex thinking and coordination among multiple sectors of society, including health, education, labor, agriculture, business, justice, law, defense, politics and of course, the media. Only with the positive impact from all fronts can we expect a reduction of suicides and only if all sectors adequately address lack of awareness of depression, anxiety, and suicide. Think of suicide as a fast-moving disease like Ebola or West Nile Virus. It's on television so often, people take precautions, listen, read and remember how to avoid being a victim. Same huge effort needs to be televised, presented in class, church, sports field and at home. Conversation needs to be held all the time to knock the catastrophic results out of our present and future. We read about the tragic deaths of young people ingesting opioids for kicks, for attempts at popularity, for emulation, bravery or any other reason. Suddenly they are dead and weren't even hooked on any drug before or during.

There has been so much taboo thinking, stigma attached to mental health or embarrassment surrounding depression, anxiety, and suicide, it has been moving at a snail's pace for prevention. Why doesn't the country see that mental health is no different than physical health? That it's ok to seek treatment without negative feedback.

If we teach coping skills with projects in elementary school, middle school and high school, resilience can overcome many mental problems right off the very start. Giving our children the option to solve the littlest problem to the biggest, or making up problems for a classful of children to talk through and decide.

Bullying in regard to clothes that some children may wear can be eliminated if our schools decide to use uniforms for regulation. Economic status would be virtually vanished. Giving the kids two choices of shoes could further regulate bullying if clothing doesn't do it.

Teaching students the value of life, respect for others, love for all, and all things positive at the earliest level of education teaches children of all walks of life, all ethnicities, religions, sexes, color or economic status how to live without hate or jealousy. Share your plan with their parents and ask them to participate in the same positive way to help reinforce the message. They say it all goes out the window if parents don't get behind the teachers in assistance, give them the basics in writing and perhaps they will see your reasoning and try to help you with their kids.

In the middle schools, why couldn't we have work sessions where kids could sit in small groups, and with direction from the teacher, feel free to discuss what is particularly bothering them, without fear of ridicule or punishment? If a parent rejects this type of class, I feel a counselor should spend some time with a child showing feelings of distress.

If our kids are spending 8 hours a day, 5 days a week with instruction, at this particular time, shouldn't they be given the tools just to survive? Who truly, at this time, needs to read "Tale of Two Cities," or "Moby Dick"—when lessons of honesty, resilience, respect, love and kindness is what perhaps will take us forward and rid corporate and political cheating—lying- street violence- not playing by the rules?

In our homes and in school, could we not hold special sessions which deal with today's problems; as peer pressure, competition, broken homes, clothing costs, drug and alcohol pressures, sexual demands, bullies, and fears about everyday life with conditions creating tremendous worry and stress among youth?

Prayer in school being banned is so unnecessary in our own country.

Return it to the classroom and let kids from all over the world, just pray silently. If they do not believe in a higher power, let them just slow down for a moment and chill out to collect their thoughts. And what is the problem about flying our own flag? This is America. If others wish to fly another country's flag, let them do that in their house. But why did they come to America if not to respect their new country.?

Suicide should be scripted and aired. Harsh reality is what kids may need to see the consequences of their actions. Hiding our heads in the sand is deadly, naïve and dangerous in today's real world.

Consequences of alcohol and drug addiction should be spoken about openly. No more secrets about depression, anxiety and suicide; alcohol and drugs. None of these can or should be glorified, as they all are responsible for alleviating reality, and taught early enough, kids should be happy to cope with anything real and responsible. Our kids are way ahead of us so hiding consequences is pretty stupid these days.

Self-esteem courses, focus on positive thoughts and positive actions should be a course of its own. Showing negative outcomes of hatred and cruelty remain with children. Teaching perseverance and persistence builds strength of character, and allows a child to be happy with himself.

Praising our children for a deed well done is the answer. Don't praise them for how handsome, smart or cute they are; praise the action for it's the idea of the outcome. Exerting pressure to be the smartest, the fastest, the best can often backfire, setting up unattainable goals. It often produces the bully, the liar, the cheat thinking, "I'll win, doing anything I can." Just teach our children to enjoy themselves and work to the best of their ability. Teach them that in order to succeed, they must also fail to learn from both aspects.

Group sessions encourage a variety of contributions. Hearing the opinions of others, not in agreement with you, and respecting them for their point of view, is an invaluable lesson at lower grades. Handling bullies swiftly is urgent. First time, a warning; second time removal for a day; third time removal from school. They want total control. They feed on the misfortune of others who may be smaller, younger, weaker, slower or any reason and being allowed to continue sets the stage for future disaster. Mass shooters often fall into this class.

I feel it is important to assign a help-mate to a new student coming into the school at an off-time during the year to make comfortable and answer questions regarding clothes and other popular subjects to give confidence to the new student.

When I left my school in the fifth grade and moved to a suburb, girls were laughing at me when I walked down the hall. One girl I knew had already heard the rumor. It was about the argyle socks I wore with my loafers. Nobody wore anything but saddle oxford shoes with heavy short white socks. Mom took me shopping the next day and I was no longer laughed at.

Perfectionism can be very deadly. It often leads to depression because the youth is never satisfied with his work, his looks or his accomplishment in class or sports. Don't just tell your kids it's ok when they fail; show them it's ok. Ask them how they feel about the missed ball, the missed tackle, missing an A or a B. And don't just tell them to blow it off, as so many coaches have always done. When a kid is hard on himself, he may be blowing it off in public, but beating himself up inside. It's the feelings inside that are so important.

Parent/teacher conferences are common and problems may be brought to the surface. Why aren't there coach/parent conferences? Because the unwritten rule is that nobody complains to the coach, or they get benched. Big Mistake. I know. After 16 years of baseball, Mike finally complained to the coach on the way he would belittle his teammates. Mike was benched. When he quit and then regretted it four days later, and got back on, he was benched for the rest of his life, which was a mere 4 months later.

Men charged with the responsibility of handling boys need to be aware of boy's feelings and the fact that they don't willingly share things like girls do. Male teachers and coaches all need to let boys know that it is ok to come to them with a problem and not be punished for it. The old adage that boys don't cry is dead. Boys need to cry more than ever these days. Boys should now be taught that it's ok to be honest about their fears, their feelings and their need for understanding.

Are we guilty of turning our children into people-pleasers in our effort to teach them to be polite? We need to assure our kids that they don't have to please everyone. They have the right to say and feel what they believe is best for themselves.

Now that my son is deceased, I often ask myself if I made some pretty stupid mistakes along the way:

I think I worried about Mike too much because he was just so darn nice. He was genuinely good, sweet, fun, honest and forthright. He rarely complained and seemed to smile a lot and be quite happy.

I think I protected him too much because during the 1980's life became more violent

I think I missed too much because I had a demanding job.

I think I trusted too much because I knew God was good.

I think I made excuses for Mike to keep him from being too hurt.

I think I did too much for him, praised him too much and didn't toughen him up enough.

I thought I was just a super mom, lucky to have three healthy, wonderful children. Two girls-then Mike.

Only in hindsight do I suddenly realize that my responses to my child's crisis were lame.

Only in hindsight do his clues suddenly blare out to me that they were cries for help.

Only in hindsight do I realize we owe it to our children to become keenly educated on their needs, impressions, pressures and fears, in order to perceive the problem.

Only in hindsight do I know that asking the right questions might have saved the so-loved boy I raised.

What about a follow-up system when a youth quits high school or college? A simple phone call, email or text from the administration office would inform a parent about this withdrawal. Had I known

Mike quit summer school the last day in order to have his expenses reimbursed to us, I would have caught the love of our life in a secret we never knew until after he was buried and we received a refund.

If an employer would just make one phone call or text to a parent living at home, or elsewhere, awareness and intervention might well have saved their suicidal youth. Simple as it may seem, conversation and communication saves lives. Mandatory postings of the signs of depression, anxiety and suicide in every public place; in your home, your church, in the movie theaters, television, in offices and more I guarantee will save lives from unseen, unheard cries for relief from the pain of mental anguish.

There has never been a more crucial time for us to listen to our youth. Learn the life-saving warnings of death to come and intervene with a counselor, a community support group, a professional mental health physician. We are missing our kid's cries for help because we are totally uninformed, too busy, too consumed in ourselves or just plain not paying any attention. Oh, God—I just didn't even know of depression in 1994.

How many school killings, drive-by shootings and suicides must it take to convince us about the urgent need for complete awareness of mental health issues of our youth and the intervention necessary to keep our kids alive?

"It's so important for people who are hurting to know that the story hasn't been finished. Things are terrible now, but there's more to the story…"

—Dr. Richard Goodling

CHAPTER FOURTEEN

———— ✺ ————

THE IMPORTANCE OF QUESTIONING

WHILE MOST YOUTHS communicate their intentions to possibly kill themselves in words or actions, the problem is that we don't recognize their cry for help mainly because it doesn't even occur to us that our beloved child would ever think of doing such an unimaginably catastrophic deed to himself or the family he loves.

If you are knowledgable enough to see pending disaster in your youth's mannerism, get him immediately to a professional counselor or doctor because very often the youth acts impulsively. The professional starts asking questions to determine the extent of the depression, if it's accompanied with anxiety, how much the youth is not sleeping, if he is involved with drugs or alcohol, what is the cause of his tremendous stress, and is he or she suffering worthlessness and hopelessness?

If you are unable to get your loved one or friend to go with you for professional assistance, it is imperative that you do your own questioning, particularly the extent of his pain, the real reasons for her stress and indecision, and the thoughts your youth or friend may be having for ending his life. Getting involved is far better than ignoring and hoping it's just a phase.

Please know that it is urgent to pay close attention to your youth's attitude, actions, verbiage and realize that we all have bad moments and bad days, but many weeks of not coping is a message to intervene, ask questions, get immediate help and you may save this wonderful person with medication and therapy most of the time.

Please realize that mental illness is simply an ailment in the brain, whereas physical illness is simply an ailment of muscles, joints, bones and organs in the body. There cannot be embarrassment, humiliation or a secretive nature about a brain disorder any more than these issues ever exist with a physical ailment.

QUESTIONS (MIDDLE SCHOOL LEVEL)

Do you like yourself?
    Always   Sometimes   Never
Do you feel loved in your family?
    Always   Sometimes   Never
Do you have feelings of worthlessness?
    Always   Sometimes   Never
Do you share your feelings with your folks?
    Always   Sometimes   Never
Do you share your problems with a friend or sibling?
    Always   Sometimes   Never
Do you feel liked by kids in your classes?
    Always   Sometimes   Never
Do you get bullied?
    Always   Sometimes   Never
Would you feel ok about telling the bully to quit?
    Always   Sometimes   Never
Would you warn the bully that you are going to report him?
    Always   Sometimes   Never

Would you report him/her to the principal?

Always   Sometimes   Never

QUESTIONS (HIGH SCHOOL LEVEL)

If you suspect your youth is changing in looks, attitudes, habits and behaviors, ask questions and LISTEN.

It seems things haven't been going so well for you lately. Are you angry or are you sad?

Is there something you feel badly about that you might want to share with me?

Try me—and maybe I could just listen and not make suggestions or give you advice.

Do you feel like things will get better, or are you afraid they will stay the same or get worse?

Sometimes kids think they would be better off dead. Do you ever think about that?

What were your thoughts about death?

How do you think your parents would feel? What about your brothers or sisters?

What about your friends- how would they feel if they couldn't have helped you?

Has anyone you know killed themselves? Do you know why?

How often do you have these thoughts?

Is there anyone or anything that would stop you from doing this?

Do you have the means to do this at home or somewhere else?

Have you ever tried to kill yourself before?

If the boy/girl you are in love with broke up with you, how do you think you would handle it?

Can you picture yourself where you would be when you are 21 or 22?

If you don't get accepted to the university you wish, are you open to several others?

If you don't make a college team you dreamed of, what other options would you consider?

If you decided to go into a trade rather than college, would you have belief in yourself to work your way up?

If you didn't make it to the major league, would you accept minor league and work to the next level?

If you didn't pass the bar or attain your master's degree or PH. D, what would you decide to do?

Do you see yourself helping others? What type of help do you see yourself giving?

Questions (When you suspect your youth suffers from excess anxiety and/or depression for 2+ weeks)

Do you sometimes feel so bad you think of suicide?—Most everyone has thought of suicide, however fleetingly. Don't feel as if you are giving your youth the idea. It can often be a relief bringing the subject out in the open and discussing it without judgment, shock or disapproval. It shows you are seriously tuned into their stress and anxiety. If the answer is "Yes," I do think about suicide—take it seriously and ask questions like –

Have you thought about how you would go about taking your life? Do you have the means?

Have you decided when you will do this? Have you already tried taking your life? What happened?

If your youth opens up and has a definite plan with the necessary means and the time set, your immediate response should be to get urgent help. Don't, in any case, ignore or procrastinate. Go together for help.

How do you imagine I could get through even one day if you kill yourself? How could we all go on?

Discuss the reality of this as opposed to going to talk with a doctor and receive therapy and medication.

And discuss all the options available and the fact that all things change in a day, a month, a year.

And make your youth promise he will not do anything to hurt himself without trying to get help.

CHAPTER FIFTEEN

MIKE'S GOODBYE

Mike's Personal Letter of Goodbye to our Family (not dated)

To All of my Loved Ones

I am very sorry this incident had to happen the way it did. I was once set on a few goals to achieve in my lifetime.

My biggest goal was to be a Major-League Baseball Player. Certain complications took place in selection of schools, finding the right coaches, and being in the right place at the right time. My second biggest goal was set on always being a good father.

Towards the end of my life, I found myself to be quite boring, without much personality. I found that I could never really enjoy life the way it was meant to be enjoyed. I was always putting pressure on myself when instances didn't demand any strain. Life was precious and I did not fully appreciate it.

Please do not blame Leslie for this instance. Perhaps our situation of separation was meant to be so that she could find someone else. This was not done over her. I feel as if there is nothing else for me in life to go after.

I have no direction or statement of purpose. I always wanted to live my life as long as I was happy, but I do not see that anymore.

I couldn't ask for a more loving and caring family than what I had. You all would do anything for anybody, virtually almost all the time. I don't see myself qualifying under that category. I love you all so dearly, and I hope we will meet again in later life when your lives are successfully completed. Love always,

Michael J. Falk

CHAPTER SIXTEEN

WHAT HAPPENED TO MIKE?

If Mike were here today, I think this is what he might say about all of this....

"Nobody knows why. I don't even know why. But I ended my life, and they are all still trying to get over it. I don't know what happened to me, but I was so mixed up and scared of what I wasn't and more scared of what I would probably never be. I just couldn't keep pretending it was all ok. I was tired, and it hurt so much, I just felt it was easier to let it all go and quit trying so hard.

I knew it would kill my family, but I thought they would get over it. They loved me so much and always worried about me because I was vulnerable. All through my life there had been occasions that didn't call for the pressures I put on myself. Things often went over my head, and as I grew up, my friends thought I was kind of dense when I didn't understand things.

My folks and baseball coaches in grade school and middle school kept trying to make me see that my mistakes were no big deal, but I couldn't shake my mistakes off very easily. I knew I did a lot of good things, but the bad strike-outs or ball misses would eat me up. Mom always said, "Just do the best you can do." She just wanted me to enjoy the game and aim to be one of the good ones. That would take off the pressure. But she didn't understand. Baseball was my life, and I wanted to do great things.

I gave 110% at practice, in the games and was like a perfectionist. I just wanted to please my team, my coach and myself. Same thing in school. My friends would get A's and never even study. If they got B's or C's, they didn't even care. I couldn't do that. So, I worked harder and after 4th grade, got all A's.

I never liked that my mom was a "work mom," instead of a "home mom," but my dad's business failed during a recession in 1974. She sold a lot of houses and we got to go on fun family vacations. My grandma moved near us to help take care of me while Mom worked. My sisters were in high school and college while I was in elementary school, and it wasn't always easy on my parents to have two teenagers..

Everyone thought I was the happiest kid. I smiled all the time, laughed a lot, had good friends, did well in school and athletics, always trying to get up—keep up—move up—and live up to my own expectations.

My parents got divorced when I was fifteen. They stayed good friends, had the same lawyer, and I laugh thinking about the fact that it was so easy, he forgot to charge them. Dad moved to Florida when he found a new job in architecture. I wasn't happy about that. At the end of the ninth grade, I moved to Orlando to live with him so we could work out together, play golf and he could help me practice baseball. I knew that Florida was a good place to be for baseball too.

I was a "walk-on," at a good Florida high school with a top baseball team. I had a couple of girlfriends, but really didn't have much time for them, because we played all over the state, and if I wasn't on the ballfield, I was studying to keep up my grades for college.

During my sophomore, junior and senior year, I had great times. I played good ball and had lots of new friends. Mom flew down almost every other weekend and we went everywhere together, even with Dad's girlfriend. Since my sister was a flight attendant with American Airlines, we got all sorts of free passes so it was great to always be together.

I was invited to play for the Houston Astro Scouts team before I went to college and it was one of the best experiences of my life. Baseball was my life and had been ever since I was six years old. After playing ball for a college in Orlando, I was scouted to play for a school in Alabama. Not long after I arrived, I fell in love for the first time in my life. She was a beautiful, long haired, blond southern girl and I fell hard.

My life took a big turn. At first, I was amazed to see that all I had ever done before was rush to class, study every spare minute and worry about everything. Now I could think of nothing but her. I started losing interest in my studies.

I began getting really upset with our coach because he lacked respect for most of the guys on our team and favored the "kissups," which made me sick. Leslie was upset that I spent my whole life on the baseball field, not having enough time for her. I quit the baseball team, regretted the decision, rejoined the team, was benched, and then made the decision to return to Texas for my senior year in college. It all went downhill from there

In February, 1994, I filled out applications for entrance into three Texas universities. I carried a 3.6 point average, and thought I might get another baseball scholarship during my senior year. When my junior year ended mid-May, I returned home to Plano, got an internship at our local hospital to boost my resume for grad school, and started a lawn cutting service with Bill, my best friend since kindergarten.

Its June and I haven't heard a word from any of the universities. I called all three admin offices only to learn that they had never received my transcripts from Alabama. We freaked and called the admin. office, and learned that my baseball coach hadn't ever bothered to release my unused scholarship funds, and they couldn't release my transcripts until the funds were received. Call after call to the coach went unanswered.

Finally, after going to the Dean, the coach was forced to release the money to the administration office, and my transcripts were going to be sent right out. But it was now July and too late to get into any of the three universities for the fall semester. I was also unable to find a baseball team in June because they were already filled up and active in the summer session. I felt I was falling apart.

To further complicate things, Leslie decided to come to Texas and go to the university I decided I wanted. We both decided to go ahead and take a few courses in case either of us lost credits in our transfer from a Methodist college. I had already enrolled at Collin County Community College and was taking Anatomy and Computer class.

I told Leslie to hurry up and enroll at our community college electronically. She was a sophomore, but didn't dream she couldn't get in after arriving here and having the opportunity of looking at the school catalog and picking her classes around mine. She didn't enroll, and by the time she arrived, we went to 3 campuses but she was unable to get into any of her required classes.

Now, she fell apart. Her parents were upset and told her to just forget about it and come home to work until we were both enrolled in one of the universities for January 1995. I missed her and went to visit my dad in Florida and went to see Leslie in August. Came home. Watched television and told my mom and Rod I was busy studying.

They were in the room right next to me, but the phones were in constant use with other Realtors or their clients because they were in the process of selling 11 homes and swamped with relocation families. But, every day we would walk and talk about all the things going wrong in my college transfer plans, my girlfriend's screw-up not signing up soon enough when she decided to come to Plano to go to school with me first semester. And worst of all, I was unable to register for my senior year in the fall. I was lost. I suddenly had no direction. I absolutely had no purpose. It was all about timing. And every day after May 16th nothing about timing was right.

Alone, on a Saturday afternoon, September 17, I wrote a letter of goodbye. I took my stepfather's not so secretly hidden antique British revolver under the magazines in his nightstand for emergency; I crawled into their empty whirlpool tub so that I wouldn't make a big mess; I aimed the gun at my disappointed heart, pulled the trigger, and kissed it all goodbye. I SCREWED UP! I REALLY SCREWED UP! BUT IT WAS ALL TOO LATE…

Please don't consider suicide. You deserve to live. Tell a friend you need help. Tell your folks you are afraid of killing yourself. Think about your family and friends and pets and people you will meet in the future that will change your life. OR CALL:

National Suicide Prevention Lifeline at:
1-800-273-8255

Text "home" to the Crisis Text Line at 741741

or go to suicidepreventionlifeline.org

LIVE FOR YOUR SAKE AND THAT OF OTHERS

HOW MANY SCHOOL KILLINGS, DRIVE-BY SHOOTINGS AND SUICIDES MUST IT TAKE TO CONVINCE US ABOUT THE TOP PRIORITY URGENCY FOR TOTAL AWARENESS OF MENTAL HEALTH ISSUES OF OUR YOUTH AND THE INTERVENTION NECESSARY TO KEEP OUR KIDS ALIVE?

REFERENCES

American Foundation for Suicide Prevention 8/22/12

Anxiety Disorders- National Institute of Mental Health 3/19/15

AAS / Christopher W. Drapeau—U.S.A Suicide 2014 Official Final Data

Change Direction- A National Campaign-Founder Dr. Barbara Van Dahlen

Mayo Clinic Health Information

Resilience and Meditation—Time Magazine June 1, 2015

More to Life than Being Happy—Dallas Morning News—1/22/13

Identify Depression—Time Magazine—Health 3/16/2015

Ways to Teach Kids Resilience—
MomentsADayBouncbackParenting.com—Resilient Families

Comforting Friends- Outreach for Survivors of Suicide—Jared's Story/com—3/24/2001

Being Suicidal: What it Feels Like to Want to Kill Yourself- 4/12/2015

CDC's National Center for Health Statistics—2016

Suicide.Org—College Student Suicide 2/12/12

American Association of Suicidology—Helping Survivors of Suicide—2014

The Book of Life—Human Genetic Code—USA Today.com 2009

National Alliance for the Mentally Ill—NAMI facts

Accessatlanta.com/bigstory—2/23/1999 Suicide: Breaking the Silence

Scout Association—Victorian Branch—Youth Suicide Prevention 9/10 2000

Spanusa.org/Suicide is a National Problem—2/23/1999

National Institute of Mental Health (NIMH) Anxiety

The Washington Post.com- Suicide Mission—11/3/2003

Anxieties.com Generalized Anxiety Disorder—Summary 4/12/15

CPSIA information can be obtained
at www.ICGtesting.com
Printed in the USA
BVHW030750140419
R9834200001B/R98342PG545355BVX1B/1/P